HAJ WINDZOR

and the Stone of Scone

NUMQUAM QUERI NUMQUAM EXPLICARE

SID ISHUN

Copyright © Sid Ishun 2025

All rights reserved.

No reproduction, copy or transmission of this publication may be made without written permission.

The moral right of the author has been asserted.

This is a work of fiction. Names, characters, businesses, places, events and incidents are either the products of the author's imagination or used in a fictitious manner for the purposes of satire and parody. Any similarities, without satirical intent, to actual persons, living or dead, or actual events is purely coincidental.

The author and this book are not affiliated or endorsed by J. K. Rowling, Bloomsbury Books, Warner Bros., or any other rights holders of the Harry Potter franchises.

ISBN: 9798317453213

*For Sophie, for your patience and support,
and for Henry.*

— CHAPTER ONE —

The Boys Who Lived

Charles Spencer trudged across the sweeping lawns of Althorp Estate, the early morning dew wetting the toes of his boots. The estate was quiet, unnervingly so, despite the faint hum of activity beyond the gates. The last week had been a blur of faces, whispers, and the thrum of distant engines. Paparazzi, reporters and a strange parade of mourners and royal officials had come in waves, intruding on what should have been a private affair.

He paused under an old oak tree, leaning against its wide trunk, staring blankly at the sprawling fields of his estate. There was a time when he would have proudly thought of Althorp as his refuge, his sanctuary. But the events of the last week had turned it into something else, something darker. His once serene estate was now a shrine that the entire world seemed determined to visit.

As his gaze landed on the people outside his gates, he let out a tired, resentful sigh. What he needed now was time and solitude. What had happened to his family, his sister, deserved compassion, and most importantly, the decency from *them* to leave him alone. Diana – that is what she had needed, he thought, his sadness turning into bitterness. The royals, the media, the public; could they not see that they had hounded her to her death? In the lead up to yesterday's funeral there had been no apparent reflection. Even in death, it had been about the stories and the papers, not the woman herself. And of course, to them, her death was only a sidenote in the larger tragedy.

It had only been a week since the accident: the car crash that had killed Diana and her husband, Prince Charles. And yet, despite the endless waves of news reports, there was still an eerie, suffocating sense that no one really understood what had transpired. The one merciful fact about the tragedy was that the twins, Will and Harry, had survived. Charles closed his eyes, thinking of them. The boys, each only one year old, had understandably been kept away from the funeral and the ensuing media frenzy of the last few days. He did long to see them though; he yearned to comfort them, try to give them the affection that his sister now could not.

As Charles crossed the courtyard, he heard voices from the kitchen wing. Two maids were standing in a doorway, their backs towards him, their heads close together, whispering.

'I'm telling you, it wasn't an accident,' the older one, Mary, was saying, with an insistent voice. 'The future king and queen don't just die like that without something more sinister behind it.'

Her younger companion nodded nervously.

'And *she's* vanished, hasn't she? Gone ... as if into thin air. Like she knew something bad was about to happen.'

Charles stopped, the thick, blonde moustache twitching with irritation on his lip. That woman, of course, they were speculating about *her*. The rumours in the press had always swirled, with every story and insinuation about her and Prince Charles being a new insult to his sister, Diana.

'Reckon it was revenge?' the younger maid asked furtively. 'You know, for being kept in the shadows all these years?'

'Revenge? Who knows,' Mary muttered. 'All I'm saying is, things don't feel right. Not with *her* missing ...'

As he walked away, Charles simmered with bitterness. Of course, people were already twisting the tragedy into some grand conspiracy. But it wasn't the time or place to confront the gossip; there was always gossip, especially when the royals were involved. He had learnt to let it go, though now, after everything, it was becoming harder to do. However, he reasoned, he could not let himself be consumed by these distractions. Althorp needed him now more than ever, and he needed the simple, honest work of managing it. The estate had always been a place where things made sense: land, people, order. Not like the tangled mess of royal life that had taken his sister. As his grief threatened to rise up once more, his thoughts turned back to what she had left behind. Her two boys were now even more exposed without her protection. To the people who surrounded his nephews, they were heirs and princes, not children who, at this time more than any, needed family.

As he rounded the corner of the stables, something made him stop in his tracks. A horse stood in the yard, sleek and black, with a proud bearing that was hard to miss. It was familiar, unsettlingly so, as if he had seen it before but couldn't quite place where. The animal pawed the ground impatiently.

'Who brought this one in?' Charles asked, more to himself than to anyone in particular. A groom emerged from the stable, wiping his hands on his trousers.

'Dunno, sir. It appeared this morning. None of the lads know who brought it, or where it came from.'

Charles frowned. That wasn't possible. Every horse on the estate was accounted for. He took a step closer, squinting at the creature's powerful frame. There was something about its stance, the way it held its head high and proud, that unsettled him. He'd seen this horse before – he was sure of it. But where?

The horse flicked its tail and snorted, lifting its head towards the sky, as if to watch the small flock of swans that were streaking across the wisps of cloud. They had been coming in droves since the accident, the royal messengers swooping down, one after another. The public had started to notice, and Charles was weary of their constant presence and upheaval that their messages brought. With relief, he saw that today the birds were passing overhead towards other destinations, on their way to intrude on the lives of others.

That evening, after a quiet, sullen dinner, Charles finally sought refuge in the library. His wife, Victoria, was there too, pacing by the window and running her fingers fretfully through her long, black hair.

'The press were outside the gates again today,' she said despairingly. 'Do they have no decency? We've asked for privacy. God knows, they've taken enough from us.'

'They won't stop,' Charles said wearily. 'Not until they get their story.'

'Well, they won't get it from us,' Victoria snapped. Her eyes were red from crying, her mouth set in a hard line. 'I've had enough. You've had enough.'

Charles, with a heavy sigh walked to the window and looked outside at the sombre, setting sun. He was exhausted by it all – the endless prying and questions pervading inside and outside his walls. He couldn't stop thinking about the whispers, and *that* woman, who had disappeared, just like that. Despite himself, he wondered if she could possibly have been involved and if it was all as sinister as the papers suggested. Or maybe it was simply one more senseless tragedy in a long line of royal disasters.

As the evening deepened, thick, impenetrable clouds rolled in as if surrounding and shutting the estate off from the outside world. Charles observed a few straggling swans in the distance, beginning to get buffeted by rising winds. His fists clenched in anger as he watched the elegant birds, their white feathers standing out against the black clouds above. These messengers from a monarchy that he wished had never touched his family. Tomorrow, the questions would come again. Tomorrow, the world would demand answers. But for tonight, all he could do was mourn the sister he had lost, and the life he feared his nephews would never truly escape.

*

Later that night, the storm had taken hold, and the gusts of wind rushed through the stables. Interspersed between the creaking of wooden beams and squeaking hinges was the restless shuffling of hooves. The imposing black horse pawed the ground nervously, its ears twitching towards the darkness outside. It had heard another noise, a cutting and unnatural sound. Suddenly, the horse tensed, its head lifting to watch in panic as a helicopter lowered out of the churning clouds and landed with a muffled thud in the adjacent field. The blades swung to a halt, the whir fading out while the storm calmed, leaving the vicinity in an expectant and poised tranquillity.

A small, purposeful figure stepped down daintily onto the grass. After slowly looking around, taking in the sight of the modest stables and the manor house in the distance, lit by bleary, orange lights, she reached an old and delicate hand into her cloak. Pulling out a small, chrome device, she pressed a few buttons and raised it to her mouth.

'One needs a black-outer please, now,' the Queen ordered curtly. She waited a few seconds until she saw the lights outside the manor house and the one hanging at the entrance to the stables, flicker, then extinguish. She slipped the object back into her pocket and strode towards the black horse watching her through the stable window.

As she approached, the horse whinnied softly, and the Queen smiled, patting its sleek neck.

'I should have known that you would be here, Anne,' she said dryly.

A rustling sound came from nearby, and out of the shadows stepped another figure, Princess Anne. She walked briskly up to the Queen, her boots crunching lightly on the gravel. The moonlight caught the edge of her riding jacket and her tall, crooked hat. Her eyes moved from her horse to the Queen.

'Did she give me away?' Anne asked, for a second being

glib, but with her manner belying her weariness. The Queen turned, a faint smile on her lips.

'Of course, when are you ever far away from her?'

Anne's expression shifted to one of concern as she lowered her voice, casting a glance around the quiet stable yard.

'How are the boys?' she asked with urgency. 'And why are you *here*, of all places? I almost did not believe father when he said where you were going. I have been here all day, waiting.'

The Queen's smile faded, replaced by a serious and solemn look. She glanced back at the horse, as if gathering her thoughts, before looking at Anne.

'The boys are well,' she said quietly. 'They are both still with my mother. She has been keeping them safe and away from everything, everyone. However, now that the funeral has passed, we must decide their futures.'

'What will you do?' Anne asked.

The Queen walked a few steps away from the stables, placing a hand on an old, stone wall and surveying Althorp House beyond.

'I have made arrangements,' the Queen said composedly. 'Harry is to live here, with the Spencers.'

Anne's face fell.

'The Spencers?' she repeated, incredulity creeping into her voice. 'Surely not here? Look at this place, it's practically falling apart. It's not an estate fit for an heir.'

She joined the Queen at the wall and followed her gaze towards the house. After a few seconds, she turned earnestly to her mother.

'And Charles Spencer, you know he doesn't want anything to do with us anymore. Not after ... everything.'

The Queen exhaled and then said firmly, 'It's for the best. They're still his family and he'll be safe here.'

Anne wasn't convinced. She shook her head in dismay but then stopped abruptly.

'You said Harry – what about Will?'

The Queen's eyes softened, but her expression remained resolute.

'Will, especially now that he is the next in line, must remain with our family,' she explained. 'My mother took him to Andrew's earlier today.'

'Andrew's!' Anne's voice was thick with protest. 'You're splitting them up? They should be together – they need each other. They've already lost ...'

The Queen looked away, her eyes distant, as she considered once more the plan that she was setting in motion.

'This is what's best for everyone, Anne,' she said pensively. 'They need to be brought up differently. Separately. In different ways.'

Anne remained silent for a moment, watching the Queen's face. She sensed there was more to it, some deeper reasoning that the Queen wasn't sharing.

'This past week has changed everything,' the Queen said steadily. 'It isn't just our family's lives that have been threatened ... and lost. It has done more than weaken our bloodline, it has nearly broken the Statute of Sycophancy itself. We have the public's sympathy, for now, but they demand to know more. You must have seen the headlines; we cannot control them anymore. They cannot be sated, and they will not stop. We must regain control – and we must protect Harry and Will.'

Her words hung in the air. Anne reflected on the magnitude of what the Queen had said. She bit her lip, steeling herself, knowing that she must ask the question that she had heard asked countless times over the last week.

'And what about *her*?' Anne enquired, cautiously. 'Are the rumours true?'

The Queen's face tightened at the mention of *her*. She paused to compose herself. She was more emotional and distressed than Anne had ever seen.

'I'm afraid that some of them may be,' the Queen said

heavily. 'The good, and the bad.'

Princess Anne looked imploringly at her mother, not finding the reassurance that she sought.

'So, her disappearance, it is linked then?' Anne asked in disbelief. 'But surely, even *she* wouldn't have ...' Her question, her suspicion, faltered, as if even voicing it aloud would be too unpleasant.

The Queen looked up into her face, the bright moon reflecting from her royal blue eyes.

'Princes are not meant to die in a car crash,' the Queen continued in a strained voice. 'Extraordinary people should not die in ordinary ways. I do not yet fully understand how, or why, this happened. But this was not fate, it was no acci–'

Suddenly, a distant sound of a sputtering engine cut through the night.

Both women turned towards the noise, which grew louder with each passing second. Out of the darkness, a large, beat-up campervan came trundling up the narrow lane, its headlights casting uneven beams of light across the stable yard. The vehicle came to a jerky stop in front of them, and the driver's side door swung open, an empty gin bottle crashing to the ground.

Out stepped the Queen Mother, looking entirely too pleased with herself as she hopped down from the driver's seat, her coat flapping in the night breeze.

'Mother,' the Queen said, her voice a mixture of surprise and exasperation. 'Why on earth are you driving *that*?'

The Queen Mother waved a hand dismissively.

'Oh, last week when I was on the way to the accident, I bumped into Jimmy. Poor soul, utterly heartbroken over Charles. He insisted I take it – said it reminded him too much of happier times. To tell the truth, it's quite a useful vehicle to get around in, unnoticed.' She gave the campervan an affectionate pat, as if it were some luxurious carriage.

Before Anne could comment on the absurdity of the

vehicle, the Queen Mother leant back into the passenger seat and reappeared holding a small bundle.

Ginger hair peeked out from under the blankets, and as the baby stirred, a thin, jagged scar on his forehead glinted faintly in the moonlight. It was shaped like a crown, a cruel reminder of the tragedy that had befallen their family.

'Here he is,' the Queen Mother said gently, passing the child into the Queen's arms. 'Here's Harry.'

The Queen held him close for a moment, her expression softening as she looked down at him. He was so small, so vulnerable.

'Thank you, Mother,' the Queen whispered.

She carefully carried Harry down the track to the old, solid door of the manor, flanked by the other two women. She laid him in his basket on the doorstep, along with a letter addressed to the Spencers, explaining everything. For a long moment, the Queen stood there, staring down at the sleeping child.

Anne, standing at the Queen's shoulder, said emotionally, 'Are you sure this is the best place for him? Do you really want him to grow up as a Spencer? They really are the worst sort of social climbers imaginable – well, apart from the Middletons.'

'Perhaps once,' the Queen said thoughtfully. 'I know it seems strange, but he will be better off here. This family, like ours, has suffered a great loss. They will want privacy and tranquillity, two things that we cannot provide. As you well know, even though we abhor them, we need the press – we cannot shut them out. But for Harry ... he's far better off growing up away from all the paps ... until he is ready.'

The Queen Mother let out a bereft whimper and blew her nose loudly.

Anne shushed her urgently and the Queen comforted her, 'There, there mother. It's not goodbye, after all.'

With one last look down at the baby, who turned peacefully under the blankets, the Queen whispered, 'Good luck, Harry Windzor.'

She turned back to Anne and her mother, leading them away from the manor house. No words passed between them as they disappeared back into the darkness.

— CHAPTER TWO —

The Venison Class

Nearly ten years had passed. The Althorp estate had hardly changed at all, with nothing giving away the existence of the young prince that lived there. In fact, of everyone bustling around the estate, only Charles Spencer and his wife knew that Harry was actually the son of Prince Charles and Princess Diana. To everyone else, including Harry himself, he was just another Spencer cousin, who had come to live at Althorp when he was only one year old due to a family tragedy. Although he was well cared for, and was surrounded by a kind family, he sometimes felt like he was the odd one out.

Harry woke up that morning with a beam of morning sun warming his face. As he sat up, he realised he had had the same dream that returned time to time. He could never fully piece it together, but there was always a rumbling engine, the cool night air and the smell of horses. As the images drifted away, he sensed that the house was already humming with activity, and he could hear the muffled sounds of his cousins chattering, and footsteps rushing up and down the grand staircase.

Today was Kitty's birthday, and the whole family was heading out for a shooting weekend. It was one of those prestigious events that Harry rarely got to be a part of, always left behind with the nanny while his cousins went off on their exclusive adventures. But this morning, as Harry got dressed, his Uncle Charles came into the bedroom, looking more annoyed than usual.

'Nanny's come down with something,' he said with exasperation. 'You'll have to come with us. But for heaven's sake, don't draw attention to yourself. Today is for Kitty – I don't want a repeat of her last birthday. Do you understand?'

'Yes, Uncle Charles,' Harry said quickly, but stifling a smile at the thought of the upcoming day out.

As his uncle stomped out of the room, Harry was left with the usual despondent feeling from being blamed for things that were not his fault. All he had done the previous birthday party was to take the game, Sovereign Says, a bit too seriously. During his turn to give commands, he had got carried away, relishing the power he felt as the other children obeyed each and every order. Uncle Charles had come back into the room as the others were bowing and curtsying to him, treating him like royalty. Even now, Harry didn't understand why his uncle had reacted so angrily.

The drive to the estate that was hosting the shoot was long. Harry sat quietly between his younger cousins, Kitty and Amelia, who were bickering about who would get the first turn with the ponies.

'You know you'll knock over the jumps anyway,' Amelia taunted, flicking Kitty's ear. 'You always do.'

'Shut up,' Kitty muttered, trying to push her hand away. 'I'll definitely never score as bad as that one time Harry had a go on that old donkey, I can promise you that.'

Harry stayed silent, looking out the window as the green and yellow fields passed by. He was used to these kinds of comments, used to being on the sidelines. He didn't really mind though; he was thrilled to be going.

The estate was everything he'd imagined: wide, open fields lined with dense woods, and in the distance, undulating hills that looked like they went on forever. Staff bustled about in their smart, green jackets, preparing for the day's activities. Trotting around the grounds were dozens of working dogs:

spaniels, labradors, and retrievers, their tails wagging and eyes bright with enthusiasm. As the family climbed out of the car, Uncle Charles placed a firm hand on Harry's shoulder.

'Remember what I said,' he warned. 'No showing off. There are some other Earls participating today, maybe even a Marquess. I don't need any ... questions.'

'Yes, Uncle Charles,' Harry said, forcing a polite smile.

But as soon as his uncle turned away, Harry's attention was drawn to the dogs. They were lined up, waiting to be given commands, and Harry couldn't help but drift towards them. He crouched down next to a black labrador with a glossy coat, who looked up at him with intelligent eyes.

'Hello there,' Harry whispered, rubbing the dog behind the ears. 'Bet you're excited, aren't you?'

The dog let out a low, happy bark, and before Harry knew it, the other dogs were sidling up to him, noses nudging at his hands, tails wagging furiously. He laughed, feeling a warmth spread through him that he hadn't felt in ages.

'Good with dogs, aren't you?' came a voice. Harry looked up to see one of the gamekeepers, an older man with a weathered face and a tweed cap perched on his head, watching him with interest.

'Yeah,' Harry replied, patting the head of a wiry-haired spaniel, 'they just understand me.'

'Well, this one doesn't usually take to strangers so quickly,' the gamekeeper said, raising an eyebrow. 'You've got a touch for them, that's for sure.'

Smiling at the compliment, Harry then heard Kitty's voice calling out.

'Harry! Come on, they're starting!'

With one last pat, Harry reluctantly left the dogs and joined his cousins, who were now gathering with the rest of the guests.

The day's activities went as expected, with various competitions testing everyone's shooting skills. The main event of the day was the deer stalking contest. Four men were shown an image of a huge stag that lived on the estate, and they had an hour to be the first to find and shoot it. Harry had never understood the appeal of blood sports. He had once observed the shooting of partridges with mild dismay, but the idea of watching them shoot a magnificent stag made him baulk.

Harry hung back, not doing anything that would make him stick out, exactly as he had been told. He remembered a previous family day out, during a Boxing Day fox hunt, when his uncle had shouted at him. All he had done was play with one of the beagles, but when the whole pack got distracted from chasing the scent and instead bounced around Harry, one of the huntsmen went berserk, demanding to know who he was. He remembered how ashamed his uncle had looked as he whisked him away, and the whispers and muttering from the other people there. What Harry had found most strange was that his uncle hadn't so much been angry about spoiling the hunt, but merely for being noticed, and the questions that his presence seemed to have caused. Noticing with a jolt that Uncle Charles was watching him carefully – his eyes flicking from Harry to the Marquess nearby, Harry hunched over trying to fade into the background.

The next task was for the children to command the dogs to retrieve the birds that had been shot. The child who had the most birds deposited at their feet within two minutes would be the winner. After Amelia and a few other competitors had had their turn, Kitty was next, shouting directions to the spaniels that half-heartedly obeyed, meandering in the direction of the brush in search of their quarry. Harry watched the dogs with an intensity that made his heart race.

Unable to stop himself, he said, 'Come here,' beckoning to one of the retrievers. Drawing the interest of a few onlookers, the dog padded over to him immediately, sitting at his feet.

'Fetch,' Harry whispered, and the dog took off, nose to the

ground, heading straight for the fallen pheasants. The guests started to murmur, watching as Harry guided the dog back with a series of sharp, clear instructions. He didn't shout or wave his arms – his firm and confident voice was enough, and the dog listened attentively, moving with an elegance and precision that none of the other dog owners had managed.

One by one, Harry called over the other dogs, directing them towards the other shot birds. They obeyed him without hesitation, returning with the game to a growing crowd of amazed spectators.

'That's incredible,' someone uttered.

'How does he do that?' asked another.

Kitty's face had turned red with jealousy, as she brushed bitter tears from her eyes. Charles stood apart from the group, his face tight with barely concealed anger.

After all the dogs had returned to Harry, sat at his feet with a mound of birds, the crowd gave a polite but bemused smattering of applause. The events carried on, and Harry once again tried to blend in with the crowd, but staying well away from his uncle.

The journey home was tetchy and uncomfortable. Harry had his head pressed against the window, gazing into the late afternoon sun and dreading the impending argument with his uncle.

Aunt Victoria tried to get a pleasant conversation going, asking Charles, 'How was your haul today, darling?'

'Not too bad – I think I bagged thirty-six in total,' he replied tersely.

'Thirty-six?' asked Kitty, clearly unimpressed. 'But last time you shot thirty-seven.'

'Yes sweetie,' Charles said placatingly, 'but a few of these were quite a lot larger than usual.'

'That doesn't matter though,' Kittie whined. 'I thought you said you'd get a record number today, for my birthday.'

'I may have,' he said darkly, 'if I had not been distracted ...'

Out of the corner of his eye, Harry saw his uncle glancing at him through the rearview mirror.

When they finally got home, Charles waited until he and Harry were alone in the drawing room before he unleashed a tirade.

'What do you think you were playing at?' he demanded furiously. 'I told you not to draw attention to yourself, and what did you do? You made yourself the star of the show!'

'I didn't mean to,' Harry protested, feeling his own anger flare up. 'I just – I was good at it.'

'That's not the point!' Charles thundered. 'You're supposed to be a Spencer! You're supposed to blend in, not stand out. We're special, yes, but we're not ... we're not royalty or anything, do you understand?'

Harry frowned, slightly taken aback by this criticism.

'But why does it matter?' he asked. 'Why can't I be good at something? I had a connection with those dogs, they really understood me. They way they reacted and obeyed, it was majestic.'

Charles took a step closer, a glimmer of fear in his eyes.

'There's no such thing as majesty,' he hissed, then turned away and stormed off, leaving Harry alone and subdued.

Harry didn't understand, not really. He had apologised to Kitty on the journey home, but this reaction from his uncle was worse than any time before. The onlookers at the shoot had not been angry, so why was his uncle so incensed? As Harry went up to his small room that night, he couldn't help but feel that no matter how hard he tried, no matter how much he conformed or kept quiet, he'd always be blamed for something, just for being himself.

— CHAPTER THREE —

The Letters from One

A quiet week went by, Harry was mostly left to his own devices, exploring the estate grounds and enjoying the summer. One peaceful morning Harry made his way down to breakfast. He could already hear the clinking of silverware and the muted conversations of his cousins, aunt and uncle discussing the upcoming school year. As he stepped into the spacious dining room, he saw them sat around the long, oak table, the golden sunlight filtering through the old-fashioned windows that looked out over the rolling hills.

'Ah, Harry,' Uncle Charles said, his voice crisp but not unkind. 'Take a seat.'

Harry slid into the chair at the far end, as he always did, disconcerted by the way his uncle had addressed him and the coy way that his cousins were watching him. He'd been dreading this moment for weeks now, ever since the topic of secondary school had made its way into dinner conversations.

'We've been finalising the arrangements for Kitty and Amelia's enrolment into Cheltenham Ladies' College,' Charles announced, glancing around the table. 'Of course, they'll start in a few years, but it's never too early to be prepared.'

Kitty straightened her shoulders, trying to look nonchalant, while Amelia fiddled with her silver spoon, a small smile tugging at her lips. They'd always known they'd go to one of the most exclusive private schools. It was expected. It was what Spencers did.

Harry chewed his lip, trying to summon the courage to ask about his own future. He knew he wouldn't be going to Eton – that much was clear, but he had not been told anything. Finally, he took a breath and looked up.

'And – what about me?' Harry asked, his voice a little quieter than he intended.

Charles glanced up but avoided his eye.

'We've made arrangements for you as well,' he said briskly. 'You've been enrolled at the local grammar school.'

Surprised, Harry said, 'But I didn't do any entrance exams?'

'No matter,' his uncle dismissed airily, 'I called in a favour with an old friend.'

The door to the dining room opened, and the butler entered, carrying a small, silver tray piled high with letters. He moved around the table, quietly dropping them in front of each family member, until finally, he reached Harry. For the first time in his life, there was an envelope with Harry's name on it. In fact, it was addressed to him directly:

> *Mr H. Spencer*
> *Small Room at the End of the Hall*
> *Althorp House*
> *Althorp Estate*
> *Northamptonshire*

Harry blinked in surprise. Who would be writing to him and how did they know which was his bedroom? As he went to pick it up off the table, Charles' hand shot out, snatching the letter away with a deft urgency.

'Nothing for you,' he said sharply, glancing at the words on the front before crumpling the envelope slightly as he tucked it into his pocket. 'It's probably some paperwork about your school.'

'But –' Harry began, but his uncle gave him a look that silenced him immediately.

'It's nothing you need to worry about.'

Harry bit back a retort. He stared at his plate, pretending to be interested in his breakfast, but preoccupied by curiosity and a sense of injustice. All while the rest of the family carried on as if nothing had happened.

*

The next morning, however, things took a stranger turn. The butler brought in another pile of letters, but to Harry's disappointment, none of them had his name on them. His uncle on the other hand, ruffled happily through them, dropped them on the table and strode triumphantly to the window, opening it wide and looking out happily at his estate. He turned back to the breakfast table and just as he was about to speak when –

'Argh!'

Uncle Charles yelled as something large and white swooped in through the open window.

There, sat proudly on the table, was a magnificent swan, its wings splayed regally, and its head held high. In its beak it held a crisp, cream envelope. A stunned silence fell upon the room; everyone's eyes transfixed upon the swan.

After looking at Charles, with what could only be described as disdain, it turned slowly to Harry, bowing its head towards him to offer up its delivery with grace.

Harry stretched out his hand tentatively towards the swan, taking the letter from its beak, excitement rising within him as he saw his name written on the front. Turning it over in his hand, he marvelled at the large, wax seal of a crest that he had never seen before. A shield, adorned with ribbons, had a large B in the centre and four floral emblems, one on each side. Just as Harry went to open it, Charles lurched back to the table, knocking the swan aside and seizing the letter from him.

Harry's cry of indignation mingled with the sharp hiss of the swan as it reared and flapped its wings. Aunt Victoria shrieked as it took flight back towards the window, shielding the girls from the flurry of cereal and toast.

As the swan beat its wings and surged up into the dazzling sunlight, Charles slammed the window closed with a bang. Everyone waited, shocked, watching his shoulders heaving with his agitated breathing. Slowly, he turned around, his blonde hair ruffled and tie lopsided. He and Victoria exchanged a worried look.

'Uncle Charles, what's going on?' Harry demanded. 'Why did that swan bring me a letter?'

'Shouldn't have left the window open,' Charles said casually, but there was a nervousness in his voice that Harry had never heard before. 'It must have smelt the kippers, stupid bird. I've no idea how it got this,' he said, as he went to tuck the letter in his pocket, 'but I'll take care of it.'

Harry bravely took a step forward and pointed at the letter.

'But the swan – it tried to give it to *me*. And it's got my name on it!'

Charles cleared his throat and looked down his nose at Harry, an eyebrow raised wryly.

'Swans, Harry, do not deliver letters to people,' he said sardonically.

As Harry opened his mouth to protest, Charles continued, 'As I said yesterday, please do not worry about any letters, it's simply boring paperwork. It must be some forms from your school.'

Charles looked past Harry, to his wife. 'Dear, I think it's best if we have a word about the post, to avoid any further ... upsets.'

Frustrated, but knowing that arguing any more would be pointless, Harry lowered his arm. He cast one more longing look at the corner of the letter sticking over the lip of his uncle's pocket and left the breakfast room.

*

Over the next few days, the letters kept coming. Every morning, swans circled around the house, delivering more and more envelopes addressed to Harry. Harry waited eagerly for a chance to grab one, but each time he was thwarted. He knew now that it wasn't a mistake – these letters were meant for him. As much as he wanted to know what the letters said, he needed to know who they were from. Apart from cousins that he had met sporadically at family functions, he hardly knew anyone beyond the walls of Althorp. Someone obviously wanted to contact him badly, and it was clear that his aunt and uncle were equally determined to stop them from succeeding.

Uncle Charles was becoming more flustered as the days went on. He tried different tactics to keep the swans out of the house: keeping the curtains drawn and the fires lit in all the many chimneys, even though the summer weather was sweltering. After one swan had somehow snuck into the house, hidden in a delivery of new bedding and bursting out of the large box of pillows, letter in beak, Charles' resolve broke.

Narrowing his eyes in anger at the courier, who, both surprised and amused, laughed, 'Well, I've heard you fancy folk like duck down pillows, but this is something else!'

Charles stormed out of the hallway into the drive. He shouted for his gamekeeper, who upon hurrying up to him, cast a weary look at the swan being chased around the entrance hall.

'Adey, from now on, forget about shooting the usual vermin, I want these swans, all of them, gone!'

'I'm sorry sir, but I can't kill a swan. You know better than I, that they belong to the crown.'

'And Althorp belongs to me!' Charles roared. 'I knew this would happen one day – they are going to interfere again, turn this place back into a circus, all because of …'

He stopped, chest heaving as he calmed himself.

'Very well,' he nodded, dismissing his gamekeeper, and then walked away, contemplating his next steps.

Later that afternoon, Uncle Charles gathered his family in

the drawing room. 'Pack your things,' he said, the tension clear in his voice. 'We're leaving.'

'But where? Where are we going?' Aunt Victoria asked, confused.

'We need a change of scenery,' Charles said, his eyes darting to the window, where yet another swan was circling in the distance. 'I think it's time we visited our estate in Norfolk.'

Harry's heart sank. He had been sure that soon he'd be able to grab one of the letters. There were so many swans delivering them that his uncle couldn't keep intercepting them all. But if they left, would the mysterious correspondent know where to find him?

*

But the swans didn't stop. They followed them to Norfolk, appearing at the windows, tapping on the glass, trying to force their way in. It became a kind of game between Charles and the birds; every time one appeared, Charles would snatch the letter away, stuffing it into his pockets or burning it in the fireplace. But there were always more.

After Norfolk, they fled to a house in Scotland, then to an old Spencer family property in Cornwall. Even in these remote places Harry was never let out of sight in case a swan soared down out of the sky.

Harry grew restless; the more the family moved, the more trapped he felt. But no matter where they went, the swans found them. Harry watched his uncle become more frantic with each passing day, his movements jerky and panicked, until he finally announced that they were leaving the country altogether.

'But papa, I want to go home,' sobbed Amelia, who was curled up under a thinning blanket on an armchair. 'I'm going to miss my riding lesson tomorrow.'

Aunt Victoria walked over to her daughter, stroking her hair and looking reproachfully at her husband.

'We can't keep doing this, Charles. It's not fair on the girls.'

Standing up, with a slightly crazed look in his eye, Charles said, 'We haven't any choice. We cannot let them win.'

'Let who win?' Harry asked quickly. 'Who is it that's writing all of these letters to me?'

'Be quiet Harry,' Charles ordered. 'Go upstairs and pack. We leave tonight.'

They flew to South Africa under the cover of darkness. After arriving at a secluded airstrip, they set off to Tarrystone Estate. The family huddled together in the back of the car as they sped past unfamiliar terrain, the roads becoming ever bumpier and windier as they went further into the wilderness. The house was sprawling, surrounded by miles of open savannah and hills. Looking up at the imposing house as Harry and the others entered, he couldn't help thinking of it as a prison. He wondered how long they would be here, as he was led up to a sparse, dusty room. But, exhausted after the fraught journey, he soon fell into a deep sleep.

*

A secluded week passed, without anyone or anything disturbing them – apart from the weather, which seemed to be building in intensity. One night, Harry sat cross-legged on his bed, absently watching raindrops race each other down the windowpane. A thunderstorm rolled in swiftly over the plain, filling the air with the smell of wet earth and electricity. He checked his watch. It was past midnight now. He sighed, resting his chin on his hand.

It was his birthday. He had just turned eleven years old, but he had no one to share it with. That day had been the same as the last, everyone was impatient and tetchy, especially with him, as if their predicament was all his fault. He felt a stab of loneliness so sharp that he had to blink back tears.

'Happy birthday, Harry,' he whispered to himself, the words fading away in the empty room.

The sound of car tires crunching on the stony driveway jolted him upright. Visitors were rare out here, and especially at this time. Harry crept to the window, wiping away the condensation to peer outside. Stepping out of car was a small, energetic, elderly woman. Even in the rain-soaked gloom, Harry noticed her striking coat of blue and yellow tartan. A footman scurried to hold an umbrella over her head, but she brushed him aside and marched towards the front entrance.

— CHAPTER FOUR —

The Keeper of the Corgis

Five minutes passed. Harry could hear raised voices coming from the sitting room downstairs. Then, after an expectant silence, he heard light footsteps coming up the stairs.

The door to his room creaked open, and the woman from the car stepped inside, her eyes scanning the empty, worn-out room. She was little, slightly stooped with age, but her bright and colourful clothing and her unmistakable energy brightened up the room instantly.

She took a few strides towards Harry, stopping with her hands on her hips, and looked at him with a feisty grin.

'Well,' she said, a little breathless, 'they certainly don't make it easy, do they?'

Harry stared at her, completely nonplussed, but before he could speak, she continued, 'We have been trying to reach you for weeks now, Harry. I thought that our trusted swans would deliver the letter to you, but it seems we underestimated your uncle's determination for you to live the ordinary life. But no matter, I'm here now.'

'So, you're the one who has been sending the swans?' said Harry in surprise. 'But why – who are you?'

The woman gave a tinkling little laugh. 'Of course, do forgive me, I ought to properly introduce myself, or should I say, reintroduce myself.'

She gazed at him affectionately for a moment and then added, 'It has been many years since I last saw you, and you were only a baby, after all, so it's hardly surprising that you don't remember me. I am your great grandmother, but please, call me Granny.'

Shocked, Harry simply stared at her for moment. Looking at her features, ruddy but elegant; he knew then that she was no Spencer. He felt a strange, bittersweet emotion running through him. As he tried to gather his thoughts, he stuttered, 'If – if you're family, then ... why didn't you come see me at Althorp?'

The woman gave a wry chuckle and said, 'Families are complicated, Harry, especially ones like ours. Your Uncle Charles isn't particularly fond of us. And so, we respectfully kept our distance, agreeing that it was best if you grew up quietly away from the spotlight. But, my dear, it is now time to for you to rejoin us at Balmoral.'

'Join you where?' Harry asked, not recognising the name.

'At Balmoral – surely your uncle has told you all about it?' the woman asked, baffled.

As Harry shook his head, Charles stormed into the room, his face teeming with anger.

'You've said quite enough,' he shot at the woman, taking up a protective stance in front of Harry. 'He doesn't need to know any of this.'

With a haughty scoff, the woman glared at him and said, 'He has every right to know the truth. Now is the time, as you well know, that he must come with me to Balmoral, and begin his training.'

Harry looked from his uncle to the woman, confused and frustrated. 'But what is Balmoral?'

Letting out a puff of irritation, she rounded on Charles. 'Am I to understand that Harry does not know anything about his heritage, his future?'

'My heritage – what do you mean?' Harry interjected.

'That's enough, please,' Charles said loudly. He took a deep breath and with a desperate, pleading look, he said, 'He's just a boy, can this not wait until he is older?'

Allaying slightly at the pain and concern in his eyes, the woman reasoned, 'Charles, this is how it has to be. Like his parents before him, he must learn our ways.'

'My parents,' Harry said in a timid, sensitive voice. 'Did they go there, to Balmoral?'

'Of course they did, dear,' she said kindly. She walked up to Harry, turning her back on Charles and looking sympathetically at him. 'Can it be that you truly do not know anything – who your parents were, where they learnt it all?'

'Learnt what?'

'How we perform our duties. How to harness our majesty!' the lady said pompously.

'What duties? I'm sorry but I don't understand.'

'Our family is different, Harry. We have been chosen, anointed. We must serve our country in a way that only our family has the ability – nay – nobility to do so.'

'But why, what do you mean?' Harry said, his voice now becoming more desperate and bewildered.

'Because,' she said, as if it were the most obvious thing in the world, 'you're a Windzor, Harry.'

The silence was deafening.

'What?' Harry whispered, shaking his head. 'No, I'm not. I'm ... I'm just a Spencer.'

'No, you're a prince, and I am Elizabeth, the Queen Mother, Dowager Queen and Keeper of the Corgis at Balmoral.'

Harry eyes widened in disbelief. He looked at his uncle, not exactly sure what he wanted or expected from him – reassurance, affirmation, protection? He felt dazed and disoriented. He couldn't be a prince ... could he?

Finally, Charles broke the uncomfortable stillness. 'He's not going; it'll be no good for him.'

'And why not?' the Queen Mother demanded. 'He belongs there – it is his birthright.'

'Because boarding schools are no good for anyone,' Charles disputed, his emotions rising. 'Especially surrounded night and day by all that meaningless pomp and ceremony – everything orchestrated to delirium by the Queen.'

'Never,' seethed the Queen Mother, 'insult the Queen in front of me!'

Her fierceness made Charles take a step back.

'You, Earl Spencer, do not get to decide if he goes. The choice is his.'

Harry looked between them, feeling like a rope in a tug-of-war.

'But he is just a boy, my boy,' said Charles resolutely. 'You left him on *my* doorstep, remember? He is my responsibility, and *I* will decide what is best for him.'

'This is bigger than you or me, Charles. He is a Windzor – it is in his blood. You cannot deny his destiny.'

'I don't care what's in his blood,' Charles bristled. 'You think I'd let him be dragged into that life? Look at what it did to his parents! They died because –'

He stopped himself, eyes flitting towards Harry.

'Because of what?' Harry demanded, the sound of his heart pounding in his ears.

Charles hesitated, running a hand through his hair.

'They died *because* they were Windzors, Harry. They were targeted and harassed and hounded. Never given a moment's peace. Something was bound to happen – Diana knew it.'

'But you told me it was an accident – a car crash!' Harry exclaimed, staring at his uncle, bewildered and angry.

'Don't you see?' Charles tried to explain to him. 'That car crash would never have happened if the Palace had not invited and inflamed the media obsession. Diana, the day that she entered that world, she lost herself – I lost her. She became their tool, their plaything. No privacy, no peace, just protocol, press and pageantry. I cannot let that happen to you, Harry. You are not a pawn in their games. They are not going to dictate your future, like they did hers. You deserve better than just to be consumed by duty and tradition.'

Harry had never heard his uncle talk about his mother like this before. He could see the pain in his eyes. Is this why his uncle had always shut down questions about her? Was there a reason that his parents had died – a reason that he would not, or could not, say?

'Is this true,' Harry said to the Queen Mother, struggling to keep the anguish from his voice.

The Queen Mother took a deep breath. She was subdued, troubled, and took her time to consider her answer.

'It's complicated, Harry. More complicated than you could ever imagine. Diana knew the life and role she was undertaking when she married Prince Charles. With that privilege came attention, of course. But to pretend that we encouraged the media's behaviour or would have done *anything* to jeopardise my grandson or Diana – I will not hear it.'

'I did not mean to accuse you like that,' said Charles, ruefully. 'Obviously, I – I do not blame you for that day, it's just that it was all too much for Diana. It's too much for anyone. Especially with *that woman* meddling with everything.'

The Queen Mother gave a poignant look to Charles; for once, there was a mutual understanding between them.

'It is not easy to be a royal,' she said to Harry. 'You will face challenges – I will not pretend otherwise, but we will protect you. What happened to your parents devasted us all. Even now we do not completely understand what happened during that tragic day. But this is why you must come with me to Balmoral. We will train you, mentor you, prepare you for your role in our dynasty, so nothing like that can ever happen again.'

'But – but why are you only telling me this now?' Harry asked, voice cracking. 'Why didn't anyone tell me before?'

'Because I thought it would be better this way,' Charles said. 'It's better that you grow up away from all the madness, all the expectations. You deserve a chance at a normal life.'

The Queen Mother sniffed with annoyance.

'Normal? A Windzor does not do normal, Charles. I've heard that he's been showing signs for years, and you must have seen it. I was told about the time he insisted on being carried in a palanquin around the garden because he saw a picture of some Maharaja doing it.'

Uncle Charles shuffled his feet awkwardly. 'Well, yes, there have been times where he has, err, stood out.'

'Is that why you always got mad when I did something different?' Harry asked indignantly. 'Like the time you grounded me when I kept trying to wave like this?'

Harry demonstrated an over-the-top, wrist-twirling gesture. He'd always thought it was something he'd invented, but now he wondered ...

Charles winced, looking defeatedly at the Queen Mother.

'Yes, there was that. And I must admit I didn't know what to do that time he insisted on cutting a ribbon to open his own birthday party.'

'Oh, dear,' the Queen Mother sighed, shaking her head and looking lovingly at Harry. 'It's in your blood, my dear. All of it.'

The Queen Mother gave a start and smiled broadly.

'That reminds me – your letter, Harry.'

She reached into a pocket and pulled out one of the letters that Harry had been longing for, and finally he stretched out and took it. He saw his name and address on the front, like the one he had held weeks ago, then turned it over. He peeled off the wax seal, and pulled out the thick parchment and read:

BALMORAL SCHOOL OF MONARCHY AND MAJESTY

Head of State: Queen Elizabeth II
(By the Grace of God, of the United Kingdom of Great Britain
and Northern Ireland and of her other realms and territories,
Queen, Head of the Commonwealth, Defender of the Faith)

Dear Mr Spencer,

We are pleased to invite you to take your rightful place at Balmoral School of Monarchy and Majesty. Please find enclosed a list of all necessary equipment and books.

Term commences on 1st September. We await your swan by no later than 12th August.

One sincerely,

Princess Anne
The Princess Royal

After reaching the bottom of the page, he looked up to see both his uncle and the Queen Mother watching him. He looked back at his uncle and said, 'Can I go?'

With a weary shrug, Charles said, 'If that is what you want.'

Harry went over to him and hugged him.

'Now, Harry,' the Queen Mother said gently, 'I think it is time for bed.'

'But –'

'No more questions tonight,' she interrupted. 'You've had quite a shock, and there will be plenty of time for answers later. For now, get some rest. We'll leave first thing in the morning.'

Charles looked at her but didn't argue.

— CHAPTER FIVE —

Pecuniar Alley

The very next day, Harry returned to the UK with the Queen Mother in a royal jet. As he looked through the parting clouds down at London, he tried to reconcile his conflicting emotions. He was relieved to be back home, but he knew it wouldn't be the same anymore. At least he now understood why at times he had felt like an outsider in his own family. Deep down, he had known there was something different in him and that the Spencers, although kind and patient, had seemed to find him a burden at times. He knew he would be back with them at Althorp for the remainder of the summer holiday, but for now, he was excited about what the day would bring, and what else he might learn about his newly discovered relatives.

Harry looked over at the Queen Mother who was awaking from a snooze in her reclined chair. Her rosy cheeks were glowing in the morning light and her colourful, tartan dress was creased.

Glancing out of the window she said, 'Ah, wonderful. London already – today, Harry, let's take your first steps towards royalty. I think we ought to do some shopping. Have you looked through your letter and what you'll need?'

Harry nodded. He had been staring at the letter, splayed out on the table before him, for most of the journey. On the second page he read a list of items that he needed to take with him to school:

BALMORAL SCHOOL OF MONARCHY AND MAJESTY

Uniform
First-year students will need:
1. Four sets of school uniform
2. One set of shooting attire
3. One set of formal robes for duties
4. One winter coat
5. One pair of gloves to protect from direct contact with the public (white kid leather)

Please note that all pupils' clothing should carry name tags with their position in the line of succession

Set Books
All students must have each of the following:
Debrett's New Guide to Etiquette & Modern Manners *by John Morgan*
The Prince *by Niccolo Machiavelli*
The English Constitution *by Walter Bagehot*
Cafe Royal Cocktail Book *by William J. Tarling*
Born to Reign: The Astrology of Europe's Royal Families *by Nicholas Campion*
The Way It Was *by Ian Farquhar*
The Road to Serfdom *by Friedrich Hayek*
The Principles & Art of Cure by Homeopathy *by Herbert A. Roberts*

Other Equipment
1 sceptre
1 cocktail mixer and set of crystal tumblers
1 citrus reamer
1 telescope and horoscope chart

Students may also bring a swan OR *a tortoise* OR *a pony*

PARENTS ARE REMINDED THAT FIRST-YEARS ARE NOT ALLOWED THEIR OWN SHOTGUNS

'Can we find all of this in London?' Harry asked the Queen Mother.

'If one knows where to look,' she said.

*

The car glided to a halt outside The Goring Hotel, and Harry stepped out behind the Queen Mother, trying to appear as invisible as possible. It was unmistakable how heads turned, whispers trailing in their wake as they crossed the polished marble floor of the entrance. A few gentlemen in tailored suits watched them keenly with inclined heads, and Harry could sense that the air had shifted, like they had entered a realm where everyone knew and revered them.

'Keep your chin up, Harry,' the Queen Mother said, as they passed a cluster of women who simpered and curtseyed. 'We acknowledge them by looking down at them, you see? Therefore, we must keep our chin and nose up.' She continued striding through the foyer, demonstrating her instructions with practiced ease.

Harry kept close to her, trying to simultaneously lift his head slightly whilst avoiding eye contact with anyone. He was sure that he could hear people whispering excitedly to each other and saying his name.

'We need to make a little stop before starting our shopping,' she said. 'It's noon, which means ...'

She veered off in another direction, her pace quickening, leaving Harry to hasten after her. It was only when they reached the seclusion of a softly lit bar that Harry saw someone else who looked as out of place as he felt.

A man was perched on a velvet stool, one leg crossed over the other with a glass of something amber in his hand. He had a ruddy complexion, and his eyes constantly darted around as if trying to keep track of all the comings and goings. As soon as he spotted the Queen Mother, he stood and gave a little bow, a smirk tugging at the corners of his mouth.

'Your Majesty,' he said smoothly. 'Always a pleasure.'

'Ah, Piers, I was wondering when you'd slither out of Fleet Street,' the Queen Mother replied with a wry smile. 'Still causing trouble, are we?'

He chuckled. 'I like to think of it as giving the public what they need. And, I might add, in doing so, we play our humble part in maintaining your grandeur and mystique ...'

He bowed his head before turning his attention to Harry.

'And this must be our newest little Windzor. Could it be ... the famous Harry?'

Harry felt a prickle of discomfort as the man studied him, like he was peeling back layers to find something hidden inside.

'I am Piers Morgan and I'm to be your professor this year, Harry,' the man continued, flashing his teeth in a grin that wasn't quite friendly. 'Deference Towards the Monarchs – quite the complicated subject, but I think you'll find it enlightening.'

Harry nodded, not sure what to say. There was something unnerving about the man, as if he were evaluating him.

The Queen Mother didn't seem to notice. She had taken a stool at the bar and was ordering a gin and Dubonnet, knocking it back in one motion. With a satisfied sigh, she bounced back onto her feet and beckoned to Harry.

'I'm afraid we must be off, lots to do. First off, Coutts.'

'Ah, Coutts, the grand, old money pit,' Morgan said with a hint of mischief dancing behind his eyes. 'I'll see you in Scotland, Harry. Keep your wits about you.'

Instead of walking back out onto the street, the Queen Mother led Harry past the bar counter, down a narrow corridor and out into a courtyard beyond. She lit a cigarette with a curved, golden lighter and took a drag.

'That man, does he always look so shifty?' Harry asked the

Queen Mother.

'Piers?' she replied. 'I see that you got a good read of him then; he would not be a good poker player, would he? He is, however, quite a *resourceful* journalist.'

'But if you don't think he's trustworthy then why is he going to teach at Balmoral?' Harry asked, confused.

'That's precisely why he is coming to Balmoral. As you'll learn, it's better to spoon feed the press what we want them to have, rather than leaving them to scavenge.'

She stubbed out the cigarette butt and turned to look at a gated archway in the back wall of the courtyard. Wisteria twisted around the wrought iron gate and ivy flowed over and behind it, blocking the view of whatever lay beyond. The Queen Mother rummaged through her handbag and pulled out gold bullion and looked at it happily for a moment. Then, with a knowing smile at Harry, she slotted the gold brick into a square hole in the gate. With a satisfying click, the lock sprang open, and the gate swung away from them, pulling the curtain of ivy back to reveal the way through.

'Welcome,' said the Queen Mother, 'to Pecuniar Alley.'

Harry went through first and came out into a picturesque, quaint, cobbled street. Old fashioned shops leaned over from both sides; the warm, dappled sunshine pushing through the leaves of the lime trees that seemed to conceal the scene from the outside world. There were people happily bustling past and going in and out of shops, which had such an enticing range of window displays, that Harry did not know where to go first.

'Come on, Harry, we don't need to go there,' the Queen Mother said, rolling her eyes at a squat, red-faced man that had just proudly exited a nearby shop with a medal pinned to his breast.

Harry looked from the man to the rows of medals in the window, and up at the elaborate sign above the door that read *Sir Plus & Sons – Second-Hand Knighthoods, Peerages and Other Gongs*. His eye was then drawn to the shop next door that had a hanging sign with a silver outline of a yacht that read *Knotorious – For Yachts That Make Waves*. Reeling at the prices listed next to photos of a plethora of super-yachts, Harry laughed out loud at a sales poster that said *With Each Purchase, Receive Coupon For 5% Off Your Very Own Private Island at 'Private Isles and Exiles'*.

Looking round, Harry saw that the Queen Mother had sauntered down the street and was gazing at the wine racks in the off-licence called *Liquid Assets*. He hurried to catch up with her, making his way round a group of children who were staring at a highly polished rifle in the window of *Loch and Load*.

'Oh, there you are,' she said, reluctantly turning away from a vintage bottle of wine rotating slowly on a pedestal. 'Come on then, let's not window shop all day. I've got an important duty to do.'

After only a few steps, the Queen Mother nudged Harry and nodded towards a small and discreet pub, set back in a shady corner of the street. A door hinge squeaked as a man shuffled out of the door, his hat brim pulled low.

'The Greasy Palm,' she said with a tut. 'Now don't let me catch you in there. Your aunt got into a bit of an unfortunate situation here not that long ago.'

Certain that she was not referring to his Aunt Victoria, Harry asked, 'What happens in there?'

Wrinkling her nose, the Queen Mother said, 'Well sometimes, our pocket money gets a little low and it can be tempting to earn a little extra on the side, due to our business acumen, connections, influence ... I mean really, if people wish to pay for the privilege of meeting us and learning from our expertise at networking, I'm not sure what the problem is. But, Fergie, bless her, probably didn't need to ask for half a million pounds.'

At the mention of money, Harry finally voiced a concern that had been worrying him all morning.

'Granny, how am I going to afford everything that I need

for school, I haven't got a job, or any savings.'

'A job!' the Queen Mother replied in horror. 'Don't say such silly things. Don't you worry, we have plenty of funds. And' she said, pointing at an imposing, marble pillar-flanked building ahead, 'this is where we shall get what you need.'

Sticking close to the heel of the Queen Mother, Harry followed her up the steps at Coutts. There was no mistaking its opulence and the sense of exclusivity and secrecy. The Queen Mother stopped Harry and pointed towards a large, gold, engraved sign on the wall that read:

Beneath these halls of polished gold,
Lies secrets dark, and scandals old.
The wealth of kings, the sins of men,
Hid deep within the lion's den.
Enter, then, if you're the key,
A fortune steeped in infamy.
But heed this rhyme, the price is steep,
Your soul, perhaps, you'll fail to keep.

'Granny,' Harry said quizzically, 'what exactly does it mean about keeping your soul?'

'No idea,' she replied happily, obviously without a care in the world. 'In you go, Harry.'

The clerks that greeted them all had badges, proudly displaying their absurdly posh names like Percival Haversham-Bland and Algernon Thistlethwaite. They were frightfully polite, all too eager to show the Queen Mother to Harry's vault. They clambered into an exquisitely painted golf buggy, driven by one of the clerks. As they whizzed through passageways, heading steadily downwards, Harry saw flashes of searchlights and streaks of barbed wire. After rounding one bend at breakneck speed, Harry saw with a fright that the floor had fallen away beneath them, and they were hurtling along a thin bridge stretched out over a pool of deep water. He couldn't resist leaning over the side of the buggy to look below – but what he saw made him jump back into the Queen Mother's lap.

'Watch yourself, Harry,' she said, giggling at the shock on Harry's face.

'Were they ... they can't have been ...' Harry stuttered.

'Oh yes they were,' she said teasingly. 'You saw the sign outside – with the fortunes squirreled away down here, you had better expect some serious security.' Turning frontwards she called to the driver over the rushing of air, 'How *did* you manage to strap those lasers on them? And was that a hammerhead that I saw? When did you add that one?'

'That's right,' the driver called over his should nonchalantly. 'We are hoping to add a great white to the pool too, next month. As for strapping the lasers on, that's a task left for the local state school work-experience students.'

As Harry continued to stare incredulously at the back of the driver's head, the buggy skidded to a stop. They got out and walked up to a vault, as large as a house. The Queen Mother plucked out the key, slotted it in the lock, and pushed the door open to reveal a sight that made Harry's mouth fall open in awe.

'There's plenty in here, dear,' the Queen Mother said, waving a hand indifferently at a vast pile of fifty-pound notes and gold ingots gleaming back at them. On shelves that reached up to the rafters were chests of gold and silver coins, as well as certificates and bonds stacked in dusty boxes.

But it wasn't just money. Gemstones of deep red, blue and green lay in mounds, reflecting a warm rainbow of light throughout the vault. Harry picked up an exquisite pearl and sapphire necklace that had the largest jewels that he had ever seen. But even this looked cheap compared a long, elaborate, diamond necklace that caught Harry's eye, resting on a nearby velvet cushion.

'What's this?' Harry asked, curiosity piqued.

'Ah, that's one of my favourites; it's the Nizam of Hyderabad necklace,' she said with a lustful yearn. 'Technically that shouldn't really be here, as it was a gift from another country's monarch to the Queen,' she continued flippantly. 'It is meant to be a part of the Royal Collection Trust who curate such treasures for the benefit of the nation,' she concluded with a wrinkled nose. 'But this was given to us, and we do not ask permission to wear our own jewels.'

The Queen Mother scooped up a large bag of cash and threw it happily to Harry, slammed the vault door closed and trotted back to the buggy.

Still dazed at the immense fortune that he had just witnessed, and weighing the bag in his hand, he asked, 'Was all of that ours?'

'Well, that's some of it,' she answered, laughing at Harry's awed expression. 'Though that is merely the tip of the iceberg, darling. Loose change compared to our main accounts offshore. Which reminds me, I have an errand to run for the Queen.'

Turning to the clerk stood patiently nearby, she said, 'Take us to vault 1296 please.'

They jumped back onto the buggy and ventured deeper underground. The air got colder and damper, stinging Harry's eyes. As he shielded them with his hands, a roar and a wave of heat turned them orange in front of him. He lurched round and saw a glimpse of a man hurtling upwards, flames shooting out of a metal cage on his back, before the buggy careened round another bend. Finally, they arrived at a vast, iron door adorned with elaborate carvings of swans, lions, and crowns. The Queen Mother stepped forwards, withdrawing a tiny, gold key and slotted it into the lock.

The door creaked open, and there, covered in a tattered Union Jack, was something bulky, cold and grey. Harry could see the harsh, straight lines of the large, oblong object resting under the faded flag. The air in the vault was dry and thick, and the dust-carpeted floor gave Harry the impression that the room had not been disturbed in at least fifty years.

'What is that?' Harry asked.

'Something sacred, but nothing that you need to worry about for a very long time,' she whispered, her eyes glinting with something Harry couldn't decipher. 'It cannot rest here any longer though. Like you, Harry, it belongs at Balmoral.'

'Why?' Harry asked.

'Why indeed,' she murmured, more to herself than him. The Queen Mother, more serious now, spoke in hushed tones to Harry.

'Please do not speak to anyone about this. This bank contains many treasures of untold value, but some are invaluable ... irreplaceable.'

She beckoned over a few clerks, and they began loading the heavy object onto a luxurious, golden wheelbarrow. They dutifully attached it to a second, waiting buggy which followed behind Harry and the Queen Mother's vehicle as they made their way back up to the atrium. Back at the front desk, the Queen Mother gave orders for the wheelbarrow and its load to be collected by a royal courier and sent on its way.

*

Their next stop was Garrard, the jewellers. This was no ordinary shop, but a glimmering palace of diamonds and gemstones, with velvet displays housing tiaras that once graced royal heads. A tall, precise man in an impeccably tailored suit stood at the counter.

'Well, if it isn't Her Majesty and her young ward,' the man said, bowing to the Queen Mother before leaning over his counter to look Harry up and down.

'Welcome my prince, I am David Thomas, The Crown Jeweller,' he said with a flourish. 'I have been looking forward to this for quite some time. It seems like only yesterday that your father was in here, purchasing his first sceptre.'

Mr Thomas reached down to draw up Harry's right hand,

holding it up to his eyes.

'Ah yes, you have your mother's hands. She really was the perfect model for my creations. A 12-carat oval Ceylon sapphire ... what a stunning gem – too good to stay in Sri Lanka, that's for sure – and encircled by fourteen solitaire diamonds.'

Mr Thomas' eyes glazed over as he pictured the ring, allowing Harry's hand to fall back down. Then, with a blink, he stood up straight and said excitedly, 'I believe we're looking for a sceptre today?'

Harry nodded, though he wasn't quite sure what was happening. 'Do I just ... pick one?'

Mr Thomas shook his head with a chuckle. 'No, sir. It is not you that chooses it. Instead, the sceptre chooses the sovereign.'

He brought out several, laying them out carefully before him.

'One of these should be well suited. Please, give one a try.'

Harry picked up the one closest to him, looking in wonder at the craftmanship, and then to the Queen Mother who was bobbing up and down in delight next to him.

'What does this do, should I do something?' asked Harry, feeling slightly embarrassed.

The Queen Mother grinned, 'No need to ask, Harry. You shall see soon enough.'

'It seems,' interjected Mr Thomas, 'that this sceptre is not the one to reveal the majesty. Please, try another.'

More expectant now, Harry gently put the first one down and surveyed the others. The gold on one of them had a deeper and darker colour. It seemed old but no less gleaming. Set in a recess at the top of the staff was a beautiful, green emerald. He could not take his eyes off it, and without conscious effort, he reached out and grasped the handle. As he raised it with a new-found grace, he felt a tingle in his fingertips and he stood taller, prouder.

The jeweller gasped and started to grovel before him. The Queen Mother let out an ecstatic squeak and beamed at him.

'There he is!' she exalted. 'Our new prince – welcome to the family.'

Harry couldn't help but blush. He had never experienced anything quite like it. He felt that his lungs were fuller, he was lighter on his feet and for the first time in his life, he felt assured. All of the doubt that used to follow him and the tension that he carried whenever he was in public, scared to draw attention to himself, was gone.

Mr Thomas finally got back up with a subservient, 'Your Majesty.' As he carefully packaged up the sceptre, he muttered to himself, 'Interesting, very interesting.'

'Excuse me,' Harry said, 'but what's interesting?'

The jeweller's eyes flicked up and fixed on Harry. He was silent for a second and then spoke in a hushed tone.

'I know the history and origin of every sceptre in this shop, my prince. There is no other sceptre in my possession that is steeped in more history and treason than this one. There was a crown, the finest of crowns, but after the English Civil War, it was destroyed. Butchered and defiled, much like the king whose head it sat upon – it was broken apart, the jewels sold off to fund the schemes of a mad man.'

'But who would do such a thing?' asked Harry.

'We do not speak his name,' whispered Mr Thomas.

'But not all of that crown – the Tudor Crown – was forever lost. I have searched around the world for the finest jewels to use in my designs. Your new sceptre is set with the most precious one: an emerald from that notorious crown.'

Harry looked into the deep, mesmerising surface of the green jewel at the top of the sceptre.

'But there is more ...' he continued, with a peculiar gleam in his eye. 'The Tudor Crown contained a second emerald, and it is most curious that this other jewel resides in the necklace of the woman rumoured to have crashed your car ...'

The Queen Mother, who had been watching patiently suddenly bounded forward.

'That's enough history for today, thank you, Mr Thomas. We really best be moving on; we still have lots to do.'

Harry, still confused at what the jeweller meant, went to ask another question, but the Queen Mother cut across him.

'Come on then, Harry, you'll have lots of time to play with your sceptre later, follow me.'

*

Their last stop was Harrods, where the Queen Mother assured Harry that they could find everything else that they needed.

'And' she added playfully, 'this is where we'll get you a birthday present too, I want to buy you a pet.'

Harry had never imagined someone could buy an animal from a department store, but sure enough, the Queen Mother guided him to a secluded corner where various exotic creatures were kept in elaborate cages. There were monkeys, falcons, and even a peacock, but it was a swan that caught the Queen Mother's interest.

'This one,' she declared, pointing at the regal bird with feathers that shimmered like the purest snow. 'I think we should call her Odette.'

Harry greatly appreciated the gesture and generosity from the Queen Mother but was also a bit intimidated by the bird. He wasn't entirely sure how easy it would be to have a swan as a pet.

As he took the swan in its cage to the till, Harry noticed the Queen Mother take a sudden, sharp intake of breath. She was stood still, her eyes wide and fixated on a box behind the counter. Harry could see a large, oval, scaly shape protruding over the lip.

'What's that?' he asked her.

'That, my dear, looks to me like a very rare lizard egg.'

Harry saw her bite her lip longingly.

'But surely a lizard wouldn't make a good pet?' Harry asked

innocently.

Turning grudgingly away from the egg, and walking to the door with Harry, she said, 'I've always had an affinity with lizards – our whole family does, you know. One day I think I'll get one, but let's keep that between us.'

The Queen Mother shepherded Harry into the tailoring department, leaving him with an impeccably dressed assistant, while she wandered away, keen for another pick me up.

After being measured, Harry went into a fitting room with a fresh set of school uniforms. As he stepped back out, he bumped into a boy about his age – tall, with blonde hair and a pout.

'Mind where you're going,' the boy snapped, looking at Harry's clothing. 'Oh, you're for Balmoral too?'

Harry nodded, sizing him up. 'Yeah, I am.'

After a rather long pause, the blonde boy asked with an edge of something in his voice, 'Have we met before, sometime, on a shoot or something?'

'I don't think so, sorry,' replied Harry.

Still looking at Harry with a curious expression, the boy chastised, 'Not your thing, is it? Shame. My uncle has been taking me shooting for years.'

'My uncle took me to a shoot recently, actually,' Harry said defensively, starting to take a dislike to the boy.

'Oh, good – how many did you bag?' the boy asked with a drawl.

'I was just watching,' Harry said, matching the stare of the boy. 'To be honest, I was more interested in the other activities that day.'

'Well, we'll be sure to test our skills against each other at school soon anyway,' the boy continued lazily, losing interest in Harry. 'I imagine we shall be in competing houses – House Stuart, that's where I'm headed. Best house by far.'

The tailor returned with the boy's clothes and held out a bag. With a last dismissive look at Harry, he took them and walked away.

Feeling a bit irritated by the exchange, Harry changed back into his clothes, purchased his uniform and went for a wander. He found a corner of the store selling books that was stacked from floor to ceiling. After giving his book list to an assistant, he strolled among the shelves distractedly. As he thumbed through books in a section about the royal family, he glanced at lots of odd titles such as one about alchemy by Cornelius de Lannoy and another called *Reaching for the Children* by a medium called Rita Rogers. He saw, on the back, there was a sentence mentioning the author's connection to his mother, Diana.

Harry wondered for a moment if he could meet the author, or other people who would have known his mother. He had often thought about who his parents might have been, and why his uncle had never talked about them much. He still didn't fully understand why he couldn't have been told who they were. In keeping his lineage and status hidden from him, his uncle had also deprived him of knowing anything about his parents. To Harry, it wasn't about them being a prince or princess but simply knowing about who his mother and father had been. What were they like together? What would it have been like to have had them there? The idealised image of him and his parents clouded his mind but then dissipated when he saw a small, plain book cover.

Reading the title, *A Greater Love: Prince Charles's Twenty-Year Affair With Camilla Parker Bowles*, he picked it up and then opened it slowly. As he began to read, doubt and confusion rose in his chest. But then, just as he was turning a page, the Queen Mother reappeared.

'Well, that's all your things sorted then, my dear,' she said cheerfully, not noticing the book or Harry's expression. 'How about we find a bar and get a little drinky-poo?'

Harry slipped the book back onto the shelf and went with her. He noticed that after the excitement of the day, he was very tired, and so nodded, eagerly. A quiet sit down was what he needed, and it would give him time to ask the Queen Mother a few questions that had been bubbling away in his head, especially now. They made their way slowly back down the cobbled street, through the archway and back to the bar at the Goring hotel.

After they settled in a cosy booth, Harry sat pensively for a minute, watching the Queen Mother stirring her martini.

'Can I ask you something?' he said quietly, trying to sound casual.

'Of course, my dear. What is it?'

'The car crash – what happened that day?' Harry asked.

After a searching look at Harry, as if she had known that this question was coming, the Queen Mother began.

'I will explain, but first, there are some things that you need to know.' She rubbed her eyes and for the first time, Harry noticed her age. She looked so very old and tired, like she was remembering a nightmare from her past.

'Everything changed for us that day, Harry. Our family was rent apart. Your mother and father ... they were taken from you ... but in the aftermath, we also had to make difficult choices.'

'What do you mean?'

The Queen Mother looked down at her hands as she turned her palms up, as if offering an apology.

'I'm not sure if I'm the right person to tell you this. But we had to do it – we had to split you up.'

'Split us up?' Harry said in confusion. 'Granny, I don't understand.'

'You have a twin brother, Harry. His name is Will.'

Harry stared at her in utter disbelief.

'But where is he, what happened to him?' he asked urgently.

'He survived the crash, like yourself. But afterwards, the Queen decided that it would be best for you to be raised separately. I took you to Althorp to live with the Spencers, and Will was sent to live with your father's brother, Andrew.'

Harry's throat tightened with emotion. The shock was mixing with anger.

He blurted out, 'But why? Why were we split up? Why have we been kept apart?' He felt, drained, disoriented and betrayed.

'That was not my decision and it's not one that I fully understand, even now,' the Queen Mother said with a heavy heart. 'She must have had her reasons though, Harry. She didn't split you two up lightly.'

Harry closed his eyes for a few seconds. Composing himself, he said with a quiet resolve, 'So, what happened that day? What happened to my family?'

'The four of you were on your way to ... well to Balmoral as it happens,' the Queen Mother explained. 'As I understand it, it was all quite last minute – Charles and Diana wanted to see the Queen. I do not know what the meeting was for, but she wasn't her usual self. In all her years of duties I have never seen her so flustered as on that morning. I offered my support, but she said she needed privacy, and so I let her be. I was concerned though – I sought out the Duke of Edinburgh. I thought he must know what the issue was, but he was absent. As the day went on, I had this sense that something was amiss.'

She was now gripping her hands tight together as she stared into the distance.

'And then ...' her voice caught in her throat, and Harry saw with a pang that there were tears in her the corners of her eyes, 'the Queen came running to me. She was scared and panicked ... I hadn't seen her like that since she was a little girl. There had been a phone call – someone had tipped off the press about the meeting. And the paparazzi – they were tailing your car Harry, chasing and hounding you! She sent me to find you, to make sure that you were all safe. As I hurried out, I ran into your godfather and so we set out, together, in his campervan ... but we were too late ...'

The heavy silence hung in the air, but Harry waited patiently for the Queen Mother to continue.

She took his hand with a gentle squeeze and continued, 'We got there before anyone else; we saw the wreckage and those demented paparazzi speeding away from the scene. Your godfather, upon seeing Charles, gave me his keys and chased after those ghouls on one of their damaged mopeds. I'm sorry Harry, but there was nothing that could be done for Charles and Diana. Once the ambulance arrived, all that I wanted to do was to keep you and Will safe. I didn't dare take you back to Balmoral where the world's media would be descending. I kept you both with me in the van, hidden away in the Highlands until, on orders from the Queen, I took Will to Prince Andrew's estate and you to your new home at the Spencers.'

Harry looked up, a sad smile playing across his face, 'I think, somehow, I knew that you were the one who rescued me. I often have this dream, and I always remember the sound of a rumbling engine.'

Another silence came between them for a while. Harry sipped his drink and looked around the bar. He has tired, both physically and mentally, but he needed to know more.

'Why were we chased?' he asked forlornly. 'You said that the meeting had been leaked – but by whom? And yesterday ... my uncle mentioned something about a woman interfering, and today ... I saw a book. It was about someone called Camilla. Is she something to do with all of this?'

The Queen Mother shuddered and muttered, 'Don't say her name, Harry.'

Straightening up, the Queen Mother looked around cautiously and snapped her fingers for another drink. After the waiter had served one and withdrawn, she resolutely gulped the drink then pushed the empty glass aside.

'You must understand, royal families are not perfect. I know that the public think that we can do no wrong and that it is all like a fairytale but ... well, your mother and father both loved you dearly, but their marriage was a little strained at times. I'm sure you'll learn all about it at Balmoral, but in families like ours, some marriages are more for serving a purpose than anything else. And Charles, bless him, didn't fully understand that.'

The Queen Mother gulped, before continuing, 'Before he met your mother, your father had a friendship with another woman – *Camilla.*'

The Queen Mother shook her head, closing her eyes as she grumbled, 'Entirely unsuitable you see. We put a stop to that – and by the time Charles had returned from the navy and met Diana, it seemed that his indiscretions were behind him. Unfortunately, as history has taught us, things are never that simple with Princes of Wales. It seems that she never relinquished her pull on Charles and even worse, the press began to pry. Do you remember what Piers Morgan told you this morning?'

Harry paused to think and then said, 'We use the papers to maintain the public's deference towards us?'

'Exactly,' the Queen Mother said intensely, 'but our relationship with the press can work both ways and *she* began playing them against us.'

With a jolt Harry blurted, 'The paparazzi at the crash! Were they working for her?'

Slowly, the Queen Mother replied, 'I do not know, I do not think we shall ever truly know. But you must understand that those years after Charles married Diana were troubled. People were talking about us, even beginning to question us! They were dark times, Harry, dark times.'

Harry looked down at the empty glasses on the table in front of him and remembered the front page of the book he had seen only an hour ago. Was that woman the cause of all this, the reason he had grown up as an outsider, without his parents and twin brother?

'After the crash though, what happened to her?' Harry asked. 'At Althorp we hardly ever spoke about the royal family and I'm sure that *her* name was never mentioned, even once.'

The Queen Mother sighed and then whispered, 'Some say she moved on, retired to France like most disgraced aristocrats do – balderdash in my opinion. I reckon that she's out there somewhere, biding her time, looking for a way back in. When someone like that gets close to the top, they don't stop. She wanted Charles, oh yes, I do not doubt that, but there was something else that she wanted above all else.'

Harry leaned forwards, 'What does she want?'

The Queen Mother breathed, 'To be Queen, Harry.'

*

Later that afternoon the Queen Mother stood with Harry at the side of the road. She pressed something into his hand and said, 'Don't lose this, it's your train ticket to Balmoral.'

She then watched Harry get into a car that was waiting to take him back to Althorp for the rest of the summer holiday. She raised her hand in a farewell as the car set off, and Harry smiling back at her, settled back into the seat, tired but feeling alive. He was going home for a while but, not for long. He, his sceptre and his swan, sitting serenely beside him, would soon be off to Balmoral. He closed his eyes and slept the whole journey home.

— CHAPTER SIX —

The Journey from Platform Away from the Paupers

Uncle Charles parked the car at Queen's Cross station. There was an awkward silence as he got Harry's luggage out and loaded it onto a trolley. Harry noticed a strange, lingering sadness on his uncle's face, alongside the usual undercurrent of bitterness he had come to expect from him.

'Right, this is it,' Uncle Charles said, glancing over Harry's luggage with a disdainful look. 'You've got everything? That blasted sceptre, the uniform, your swan ...'

His gaze fell on Odette cooped up in her cage, looking regal but rather indignant. The swan had been ruffling her feathers, unimpressed by the journey.

'Still can't believe she got you that bird. Typical.'

Harry grasped the handle of the luggage trolley and looked around uncertainly.

'Uncle Charles, where exactly is the platform? I mean, how do I –'

Charles cut him off with a contemptuous wave of his hand.

'You're asking the wrong man, Harry. If you think that I ever had a chance to waltz off to some royal school in the Highlands, you're sorely mistaken.' He gave a dry laugh, one that sounded almost painful.

Harry didn't know what to say.

Charles saw Harry's apprehension and took pity on him.

Clearing his throat, he put a hand on Harry's shoulder.

'Listen, you've been invited into their world, but don't think for a second that it'll be easy. The royals – they're not like us, even when they pretend to be. They'll expect things from you, things you won't even understand. And they do not forgive mistakes. Keep your head down, be polite, and for heaven's sake, don't embarrass yourself, or them.'

Harry nodded, starting to feel even more anxious.

'Goodbye and good luck, Harry,' Charles said, turning away.

'But, Uncle Charles, where do I –'

'I don't know, Harry, do I?' he said, the sullenness creeping back into his voice. 'The train leaves in ten minutes. Best not waste time.'

He ushered Harry away and sagged back into his car, finally closing the door shut with a thud. The engine rumbled to life, and he sped off without a backward glance.

Harry stood there for a moment, feeling lost. He glanced around the crowded station, swarming with commuters, none of whom seemed even remotely interested in helping a boy and his swan find a royal train. A quiet panic started to set in – what if he missed it? What if he couldn't find the platform? He pushed his trolley forwards aimlessly, hoping something would jump out at him, but all he saw were normal platforms, and signs showing mundane destinations like Birmingham, Bristol, and Manchester. Not a hint of anything even remotely royal.

And then, as he was starting to despair, he caught sight of a family rushing through the crowds. A bold, red-haired woman with a vibrant, infectious energy was ushering two girls along with far more luggage than Harry could imagine any reasonable person needing.

'No, Beatrice, keep your chin up! Remember what I said, you need to exude confidence! Eugenie, darling, don't look so forlorn, you'll have your turn soon enough,' the woman said.

Harry knew that they must be going to the same place as

him. Gathering his courage, he hurried over, Odette hissing irately as the cage bumped against his legs.

'Excuse me,' he said shyly, and the woman turned around with a bright smile.

'Hello there! You must be another one for Balmoral, hmm? Got that look about you,' she said, giving Harry an appraising glance. 'I'm Sarah, but everyone calls me Fergie, and these are my girls. Beatrice is off to Balmoral for the first time, like you, I expect.'

She gestured towards the older girl, who had auburn coloured hair and was looking around excitedly. 'And this is Eugenie, who's not quite old enough yet.'

Eugenie, a year or so younger than Harry, gave him a bashful wave, half-hiding behind her mother's coat.

'I – I'm Harry,' he said, a little unsure. 'I'm trying to get to a special platform. But I'm not quite sure where it is.'

Fergie let out a hearty laugh.

'Ah, yes, it's not just any old platform, you know. You're looking for Platform Away from the Paupers. Only those of us with the right kind of breeding can find it.' She gave him a wink, and Harry felt a blush rise to his cheeks. 'There's a gate right around the corner, see? It looks like an ordinary bit of railing, but there's a guard. You have to walk up to him with a certain, regal air – a bit of a swagger, really. That's the trick. Shows him you belong.'

'Swagger?' Harry repeated, feeling even more lost. He'd never been particularly good at looking noble or confident. The idea of having to do it in front of strangers made his stomach twist uncomfortably.

'Yes, darling. You know, head high, shoulders back, bit of a strut,' Fergie demonstrated, swaying her hips dramatically and lifting her chin. 'Think you're a king or queen, and you'll be fine. But don't slouch. Royals never slouch, not even when they're running late!'

Harry looked from her to Beatrice, who was already

practicing her walk, a determined look on her face.

'You can do it,' Beatrice said encouragingly. 'Look, it's easy!'

'Well, come on then, let's not dawdle!' Fergie urged, and they all pushed their trolleys towards the gate. There stood the guard, dressed in a rather impressive-looking uniform of red and gold, surveying the passing crowd with a haughty air.

One at a time, Fergie and the girls walked up to him, tossing their hair theatrically as they strode past – the guard tipping his hat and letting them through.

Harry took a deep breath, adjusted his grip on the swan cage, and tried to copy the way Fergie had shown him. Head high, shoulders back. He moved forwards with as much dignity as he could muster. The guard looked down at him, his eyes narrowing for a moment, and Harry feared he'd be sent away. But then, with a barely perceptible nod, the guard stepped aside, and Harry slipped through the gate, letting out a sigh of relief.

On the other side was Platform Away from the Paupers, with its old-fashioned ironwork and signs painted in deep royal blues and purples. And waiting on the track, shining in the morning sun, was the Balmoral Express, the majestic train that would carry them to the Scottish castle.

The platform was heaving with parents and children, saying their farewells and boarding the train. After Fergie had bid Beatrice goodbye, she and Harry weaved their way through the crowd towards the train. Inside, they found a compartment, dragging their luggage behind them.

As the train jerked to life and began to roll forwards, Harry watched the platform fade away, obscured by the billowing smoke. This was it. He was off to Balmoral; there was no turning back now.

He settled into the soft, plush seat of the train, excited at what the day would bring. Beatrice, with her warm smile and an air of natural curiosity, didn't waste any time.

'So, Harry, is it? How far down the line of succession are you? My father is Prince Andrew, so that makes me fourth!'

Uncertain of the answer or how to respond, Harry said, 'Err, I'm not sure really. My father was a prince too, but he's dead, so I don't really know what that means for me.'

Beatrice's ebullience dissipated as she looked sadly at Harry.

'I'm sorry to hear that, but if it makes you feel any better, that makes you one place closer to the throne.'

Harry looked back at her but didn't answer.

Beatrice continued, 'I'm sorry, I didn't mean to be unkind. Can I ask, who was your father? I know the royal family tree is rather big, but I bet I know of him, even if he is a distant third cousin or what have you.'

Harry hesitated, he was still coming to terms with who he was and the fact that his mother and father had been a prince and princess – *the* prince and princess. But, looking at Beatrice's friendly face he realised that it would be a relief to talk about it with someone.

'My father,' he said heavily, 'was Prince Charles and my mother was Princess Diana.'

Beatrice's mouth fell open in realisation.

'No way, I should have realised!' she said, practically bouncing in her seat. 'You're *that* Harry. I've heard all about you! I thought it was rumours, you know, because everyone says they know a secret Windzor. But you're actually him!'

She looked at him blushingly and asked, 'Can I see it?'

'See what?' Harry asked, although he already had a fairly good idea of what she meant.

'Your scar,' Beatrice said eagerly. 'The one you got when ... you know ... everyone says it's shaped like a crown.'

Harry, still self-conscious about it, dithered then obliged. He pulled back his ginger hair, revealing the thin, pale lines, curved on the bottom and jagged at the top.

Beatrice gasped. 'Wow,' she breathed.

Just then, the compartment door slid open, and the trolley

lady greeted them, pushing a cart overflowing with all manner of extravagant treats.

'Anything from the trolley, your highnesses?' she asked with a small courtesy.

Harry, remembering the full bag of money he'd collected at Coutts, felt a surge of excitement.

'I'll take the lot,' he said impulsively.

Beatrice giggled but looked longingly at the moneybag.

Standing up to gather his haul, Harry saw that these sweets were like nothing he had seen before. There were Imperial Mints that looked like dusty green marbles; Bertie's Every Flavour Shots which were small tumbler-shaped jelly sweets, the box listing flavours such as amaretto and spiced rum; Liquorice Bonds were flat, black, edible bank notes. Harry and Beatrice gleefully tried each of these in turn, watching the countryside roll past and chatting. After they had eaten most of their way through the sweets, Harry tried a Chocolate Pog.

These flat discs of chocolate were decorated with engravings of an image of a royal on one side and a description in small, embossed letters on the back. Harry unwrapped one, and to his amazement, the Pog featured none other than Prince Charles. Harry studied the face, for the first time taking in his father's features. After a quiet moment tracing the lines on the disk with his finger, he flipped it over. The description on the back read:

Prince Charles
1948-1983
Died in a tragic car crash along with Princess Diana.
Previously he was Royal Patron of the Faculty of Homeopathy,
Member of the Magic Circle, he was awarded an honorary law
degree by Nazi SS veteran Peter Savaryn, he achieved a 2:2 in
History and collaborated with his mentor Laurens van der Post on
alternative medicine and the legendary powers of historical artefacts.

'Who did you get?' Beatrice asked, showing off her chocolate, which had Edward VIII's image on it.

'Prince Charles,' Harry replied, showing her. 'I didn't know he did homeopathy.'

'Oh yes,' Beatrice said earnestly. 'Our family are very interested in alternative medicine. The Queen herself says it's the future.'

As Harry tried to decide if she was joking or not, the compartment door slid open again. In strolled a girl with blonde hair, piercing eyes, and an air of confidence that made it clear she was accustomed to getting her way.

'I wondered where you had got to, cuz,' she said to Beatrice but then freezing when seeing Harry. 'So, the rumours on the train are true – I should have known you'd find him first Bea,' she teased, glancing back at Beatrice.

The girl folded her arms and gave Harry an appraising look.

'I'm Zara Phillips; my mother is Princess Anne, which makes me your cousin, like Beatrice,' she said formally.

'Hi,' Harry said back, smiling, although he could tell Zara was sizing him up. 'Nice to meet you.'

Zara shook his hand approvingly. 'You're all right, then,' she said as though Harry had passed some sort of unspoken test. 'You both might want to start changing soon. We're nearly at Balmoral, and they'll expect us in our best attire.'

Harry blinked. 'What do you mean?'

'Oh, of course,' Zara replied, looking slightly amused. 'I guess you have never really had the chance to come to royal functions before, have you?'

Harry shook his head.

'Well, better get used to it,' she chuckled. 'You'll need your kilt. It's tradition for all first-years to arrive in full Highland dress. The Queen's got a thing about traditions – especially when it comes to Balmoral,' Zara said over her shoulder as she left them, as though that explained everything.

Discovering some extendable vanity curtains in their

compartment, Harry and Beatrice divided the space and began to change into their outfits. Harry's kilt was a deep purple with gold threads running through it. He fumbled with the unfamiliar fabric, feeling a bit ridiculous. Folding away the curtains, Harry shyly looked for approval.

'Well, look at you,' Beatrice said encouragingly. 'You'll fit right in.'

Sitting back down, Beatrice began tapping her hands on her knees in boredom but then looked at her bag gleefully, remembering something. She opened the top and pulled out a strange, rotund creature and plopped it onto the seat beside her. It's wide, glossy eyes rolled eerily side to side.

'Meet my Furby, Stabbers,' Beatrice announced.

Harry stared down at it. Its body had red fur, with gold buttons running down the middle, and it sat perched on two large black feet. Its face was the most striking, with a gold strap across its chin securing a tall, black, fluffy hat. Protruding from underneath were the two staring eyes and a sharp, yellow beak, slightly parted to reveal a small, red tongue. Clasped to its side was a miniature silver sword, the hilt complete with a curved handguard, and the thin blade extending to a piercing point.

Harry blinked at it. 'Stabbers?'

'Yep, I know, it's a bit of a funny name, but that's what it was called when I was given it for my birthday. He can talk and everything – he gives me tips on how to be a good royal.'

'What, like, to be careful who you turn your back on?' Harry said sarcastically, still watching the disconcerting toy warily.

'Oh, so you've been reading the Debrett's etiquette book too?' Beatrice said happily, completely oblivious to Harry's misgivings. 'That's right, nothing is considered ruder than to turn your back on the Queen.'

The toy's plastic beak clicked, and one ear twitched. Odette woke up, opening an eye and unfurling her neck to look at it, letting out a hiss of disapproval. Harry put his fingers through Odette's cage and stoked her neck, reassuring her.

Beatrice picked Stabbers up, brushing its fur affectionately, but then looked up with a jump as the compartment door slid open with a thud.

A sly, blonde boy entered, two larger boys skulking behind him; Harry remembered him from the tailors.

'Well, well, if it isn't my little twin brother,' the boy drawled, a sneer curling his lips.

A jolt of realisation ran through Harry. This is who the Queen Mother had told him about, and he had met him not long before that conversation with her! Taking a split second to look at his twin now, he saw the familiar features like last time, but now they registered with him.

'Hello again, so you must be Will,' Harry replied coolly, refusing to be intimidated. 'Pleased to meet you. And you are?' Harry said, looking over Will's shoulder.

Gesturing to the boys who had moved forwards to flank him, Will said, 'This is Tom and Ed Lascelles, two old friends of mine.'

Harry nodded at them but kept his eyes on Will.

Will then turned his attention to Beatrice. 'Oh, I should have known you'd be here too. Although I had almost forgotten that you were enrolling this year. Why am I not surprised to find you already trying to ride the coattails of your betters – just like your mother, you've always been good at finding a free lunch.' He looked with contempt at the sweet wrappers strewn across the seats.

'You do realise,' he continued, 'that even this forgotten prince is further up the line of succession than you?'

Beatrice's face flushed a deep red, and she looked like she might say something, but Harry cut in.

'You know, Will, there's no need to be insecure, I'm sure no one can challenge your position for the throne ...'

Will's smirk vanished and something threatening blazed in his eyes as he took a step towards Harry.

'Oh, little brother – you just discover that you are a royal, and already, you are getting ideas above your station. Well, as our dear cousin here shows, it's easy to be left behind. We true Windzors aren't fools, there's a reason why Prince Andrew took me for his ward and left poor Beatrice to wallow with Fergie. You're going to have to decide very soon, who here are the heirs and who are the *spares*.'

Will spat the last word with disgust and continued to stare intensely at Harry.

'Choosing the right friends at Balmoral is of vital importance. I can help you. I can tell you who will help and who will hinder your ascent.'

Meeting his brother's gaze, Harry replied firmly, 'I'd rather decide for myself what makes a good royal, thanks.'

Will's nostrils flared. 'Suit yourself, but when the time comes, and you're ready to join the real royals, you'll know where to find me.'

Suddenly, a shrill, singsong voice rang out.

'If a prince needs to flee some scandalous claims, then hop on that jet to Little Saint James.'

With a start, Will turned to look at where the noise had come from and recoiled in revulsion at the toy. Stabbers' beak closed with a clack and its eyes whirred to a halt, staring straight at Will.

'What ... is ... that ...' Will said slowly and with utter contempt. 'Is that all Fergie can afford to get you for your birthday, a toy for commoners? Dear, dear, see what I mean, Harry?'

He turned sharply and left, Tom and Ed shuffling after him.

'Thanks,' Beatrice whispered, looking at Harry with admiration. 'No one's ever stood up to him like that.'

Harry shrugged, feeling a bit dazed by the encounter. Remembering the warnings his uncle had given him at the station, he was starting to understand what he was getting into.

The train began to slow, and Zara popped back into the compartment, along with a timid looking boy.

'We're here,' she announced. 'Oh, and Harry, I thought I'd introduce you to my twin, Peter.'

Harry laughed, 'Another cousin? Nice to meet you Peter,' shaking his hand.

'Hi Harry,' Peter said. 'You haven't seen my tortoise have you? I've lost him again.'

Zara rolled her eyes, muttering, 'How on earth do you lose something that moves that slowly?'

They stepped off the train and found themselves in a quaint and charming Scottish village, nestled at the base of rolling hills. Waiting for them was the Queen Mother, looking as regal as ever, in her tweeds and pearls.

'First-years, gather round!' she called, her voice carrying over the excited chatter of the students. 'It's time to head to the castle.'

They walked out of the village, towards the edge of a glistening loch, the clear night sky perfectly reflected on its still surface. Harry climbed into one of the swan-shaped pedalos alongside Beatrice, Zara and Peter. The mist curled around them like the folds of a velvet cloak. In the distance, he could see the spires of Balmoral rising up, an impressive and imposing structure that seemed to be calling him home.

— CHAPTER SEVEN —

The Heralding of the Houses

The pedalos came to a stop at the bottom of a sweeping lawn that led up to the castle entrance. A subdued anticipation had enveloped the new arrivals. The only sound that disturbed the serene, late summer evening was the lapping of the water on the loch shore. Harry stepped onto the grass, staring up at the massive stone castle, with its turrets, battlements, and ivy-covered walls.

The front doors opened with a creak, and there stood a tall, severe-looking woman with greying hair tied up in a tight bun. She wore an immaculate tartan sash across her blazer and surveyed the students lining up before her.

'Welcome to Balmoral,' she said briskly. 'I am Princess Anne, the Princess Royal. You are about to begin your education in royal etiquette, history, and the preservation of your social superiority. But, before you take your place with us, and learn our ways, you shall undergo your investiture. You will be placed into one of our four houses, each founded by a monarch of great distinction. You will belong to house Stuart, Tudor, Hanover or Plantagenet. Each one representing a great royal lineage with its own strengths and values.'

A few of the first-years exchanged nervous glances, while others, like Beatrice, simply beamed with enthusiasm.

Princess Anne then led them into the cavernous entrance hall, past the wide, marble staircase and towards a set of enormous, gilded doors that opened inwards to the Ballroom.

Four long tables stretched across the room, packed with older students who eyed the newcomers with a mix of curiosity and indifference. At the far end, an opulent, golden table stood where the Queen herself sat, surrounded by other senior royals in richly embroidered regalia. She didn't seem to be paying much attention to the first-years; instead, she was adjusting the cuff of her white gloves, the epitome of regal boredom.

In front of the top table, where all eyes now turned, were four curious sets of items displayed in a row: a sword embedded in a large stone; a plush, velvet cushion resting on a carved, wooden stool; a golden pin beside an elaborate goblet; and a military jacket folded neatly beside a large pile of medals.

'Your challenge,' Princess Anne announced, 'is to discover your legacy by facing these four trials. They will test you for the qualities that match our four historic houses. You may attempt any that you wish, but you will find that you can only succeed at one. You will ultimately belong to the house where your true strength lies.'

Princess Anne took her seat at the top table as the Royal Herald marched into position in front of the four strange items. The man was dressed in an ornate tabard, emblazoned with the Balmoral school crest on the front. The crest had a shield divided into four quarters, each with the symbol and colours of the four houses. There was a yellow and green spring of broom for the Plantagenets, a red and white Tudor rose for the Tudors, a silver and purple thistle for the Stuarts and a black and gold oak leaf for the Hanovers.

He bowed low to the Queen, then unfurled a scroll, paused for effect, and then in a booming voice, read aloud:

> *'Balmoral! Balmoral! The greatest of schools,*
> *Where the royals are mighty, and commoners fools!*
> *From castles and palaces, we come to be taught,*
> *By tradition and legacy, by battles once fought!*

THE HERALDING OF THE HOUSES

For the Tudors, we hail, shrewd and so bright,
Passionate and clever, their minds sharp as night.
The Stuarts so proud, cunning, and keen,
Rulers of kingdoms, yet always unseen.
The House of Hanover, steadfast and true,
Their pragmatic ways shine through and through.
And then there's Plantagenet, gallant and grand,
Regal in spirit, the finest in the land!
The Crown bestows its noble test,
Your skill and blood will determine your crest.
And so, step up, prove your worth,
It takes more to be a royal, than an accident of birth.'

When the song ended and the applause faded out, Princess Anne gestured for the first student to step forwards. A lanky boy walked confidently to the sword. He strained, sweating, but couldn't budge it. Dejected, he put on the military jacket, as Princess Anne explained, in a commanding voice, that he had thirty seconds to attach all the medals to the jacket, and that none should fall off for a further thirty second salute.

Dexterously, the boy pinned the medals in neat rows until the entire front of the jacket was covered, and he then stood motionless in a proud salute. A cheer went up from the Hanover table, and the boy basked in relief as he joined them.

Then came Beatrice's turn. Without hesitation, she went straight to the plush cushion; she sat on it, curious and patient. The hall was quiet, as Princess Anne surveyed Beatrice's face keenly for any betrayal of discomfort. But after a few more seconds passed, with Beatrice expectant but untroubled, Princess Anne shook her head and motioned for Beatrice to try another task.

Beatrice turned to her left and laid her hand on the hilt of the sword and pulled. After a few moments of struggle, it slid out cleanly. The Plantagenets applauded, delighted to gain their first new member.

Will then stepped forwards, going straight for the needle and chalice. Harry, unsure of what would happen next, winced when Will drew up the golden pin and pricked his fingertip. All eyes watched his outstretched finger, held steadily above the chalice. A drop of blood fell, and in an instant, the goblet turned from the warm colour of gold to a striking blue. The Stuarts applauded, with some students shouting and beckoning their newest 'blue blood' to their table. With a quick, satisfied glance at Harry, Will went smugly over to his seat.

A small girl with long, black hair went next, taking a second to survey the items before sitting confidently on the cushion. After a brief moment she bounced back off it, looking disgruntled and complaining of its discomfort. As she gesticulated, the Tudors applauded, and then with a smile of realisation she bounded towards them.

Then, with a gentle nudge from behind, it was Harry's turn. He stepped forwards, his legs shaking beneath him. As he walked forwards, he saw the Queen watching him from behind steepled fingers. The four objects loomed before him, each more daunting than the last. He started with the velvet cushion, sitting down and trying to stay calm. He looked at Princess Anne, but her expression was inscrutable. He wondered what that girl had felt, would it hurt? But nothing happened … there was no prickling sensation, no lump or bump. After thirty seconds, Princess Anne shook her head and motioned for him to try another.

Harry's stomach twisted into knots. What if he wasn't suited to any of them? What if he truly was just a Spencer after all? He moved to the military jacket, praying that maybe this would be the one. He began to quickly fix the medals to his front, but, as he reached for the sixth or seventh medal, the first two fell off and landed on the stone floor with a clatter. He scrambled to pick them up, causing the rest to tumble off, the jangling echoing with mocking laughter reverberating around the room. He looked around, panicking. That was his second try, and he still hadn't found a house. What would they do if he failed all four – would he be sent home? Would the Queen herself order him out?

He moved towards the sword, feeling more desperate with each step. He grasped the handle with both hands and pulled, but it didn't move. He tightened his grip, sweat dripping down his brow, and tugged again, harder this time. It shifted, just a little. And then, with one final heave, the sword slid free. A huge cheer erupted from the Plantagenet table, and Harry smiled, feeling a rush of relief and pride.

As he stood there, breathing heavily, a sharp sting ran through his hand. He looked down and saw a thin line of blood where he'd accidentally cut himself on the blade's edge. One tiny bead dripped from his finger and landed in the goblet below. To his shock, the liquid inside turned a deep, rich blue but the goblet was unchanged. Harry glanced around nervously, but no one else seemed to have noticed, they were too busy cheering and clapping. He hurriedly wiped his hand on his kilt and made his way over to the Plantagenet table.

With the pressure now passed, Harry eagerly watched the remaining students face the challenges. He applauded heartedly as Zara and Peter Phillips joined him and Beatrice at the Plantagenet table.

Finally, when the last student had joined their house, the Queen got to her feet, raising her hands to call for silence.

'Welcome to Balmoral,' she announced. 'You have all found your rightful place among the great houses of Tudor, Stuart, Plantagenet, and Hanover. You each have much to learn and to prove, but for now, let the feast begin!'

The feast that was served was like nothing Harry had ever seen before, not even at the most extravagant Spencer family gatherings. Golden platters shimmered under the candles overhead, each heaped with steaming dishes of all sizes and aromas. The first plate to pass him had foie gras arranged in intricate, gold-leafed swirls, and beside it lay a platter of meaty parcels, each skewered with a miniature Union Jack flag.

'What are those?' Harry asked Zara, who was piling her own plate high.

'Dormouse dumplings!' she replied greedily. 'Quite rare, you know. Can only find them in the oldest corners of the estate.'

Harry hesitated but eventually took one, trying to ignore the uncomfortable feeling stirring in his stomach. He had to fit in, after all. As he took a bite, the rich and sweet, gamey flavour filled his mouth, and he felt an odd sense of guilt creep in. He forced a smile at Zara, who grinned back at him.

The courses continued – each one more decadent than the last. Great-crested newt fritters were served on dainty porcelain plates, their tiny limbs still visible in the golden batter. Otter tail twizzlers were brought next, each one garnished with a slice of truffle and a sprinkling of caviar. After that, there were steaming puffin pies. Harry tried a bit of everything, trying not to think too hard about the creatures he was eating. Looking around, Harry was slightly perturbed, not only by the quantity and extravagance of the food, but by everyone else's appetite and indifference. Was this how they ate every day?

As Harry reached for a goblet of something sparkling and fragrant, he glanced up at the top table. He saw Piers Morgan, fiddling absent-mindedly with a camera, and next to him was an old man, with long, white, wispy hair drooping over a thin face with watery eyes.

Harry felt a sudden, sharp twinge in his scar as their eyes met. The professor's expression was blank, but his gaze seemed to pierce right through Harry, as if evaluating him and finding him lacking.

'Who's that?' he whispered to Beatrice.

Following Harry's eyeline, Beatrice sighed, 'Oh, surely you know who that is – it's Prince Philip, the Duke of Edinburgh.

He's the Queen's husband – our grandpapa! Don't call him that though, he prefers that we stick to proper titles. You'll see what he's like during Mixology.'

Harry turned back to his table, trying to shake off the ache in his forehead, but fortunately his attention was taken by the arrival of dessert. Towering trifles, topped with spun sugar and edible diamonds, were accompanied by perfectly sculpted crème brûlées with tiny wafer crowns on top. Each dish had a name written in elaborate icing: *Commoner's Crumble*, *Serf's Soufflé* and *Taxpayer's Tart*. Harry cringed, picking up a slice of the latter. It tasted of golden syrup but had a bitter aftertaste.

As the students finished their puddings, the Queen rose from her seat once more, and the Ballroom fell silent. She stood, impressive and poised, her crown glistening in the candlelight.

'Welcome to a new year at Balmoral,' she began, her voice carrying the weight of centuries of tradition. 'We are a school of excellence, a school for those of royal blood and noble spirit. We expect each of you to uphold the dignity of your houses and bring honour to the royal family.' Harry shifted in his seat, feeling a little out of place as she continued.

'I implore you all to avoid scandal,' she said with a raised eyebrow, 'and, of course, avoid any unnecessary contact with the public.' There was a polite tittering of laughter from some of the students.

'Furthermore, I'm pleased to introduce our new Professor of Deference Towards the Monarchs, Mr. Piers Morgan,' she said, gesturing towards the smirking man at the end of the table. 'He will be teaching you the delicate art of managing our relationship with the press.'

The students clapped politely, though Harry noticed that some seemed less enthusiastic about this announcement.

The Queen continued, 'Our caretaker, Michael Fawcett, has asked me to remind you all that the Ballochbuie Forest on the estate is strictly out of bounds to all students. As is the East

Wing, where we keep our more ... delicate treasures. Any student found trespassing will be top of the list for the next leisure centre ribbon cutting.'

A collective shudder ran through the room.

'And now, it is time for you all to retire to bed – pip pip.'

Above the scraping of benches, Harry heard prefects calling for the first-years to follow them to their house dormitories.

Harry and the other new Plantagenets were led up to one of the towers, ascending sweeping staircases lined with paintings depicting knights, kings, and historical battles. They stopped in front of a large portrait of Queen Victoria, sat in a reclined position.

'Password,' she said in a warbling, female voice, emanating from the painting, its mouth opening and closing robotically, as if controlled by a lever.

The prefect said clearly, 'Alpha Draconis.'

The portrait swung open, revealing the entrance to the Plantagenet common room. It was spacious, with plush yellow and green furnishings, tapestries hanging from the walls, and a crackling fire in an enormous hearth. The ceiling was painted with a mural of the Battle of Agincourt, and a chandelier made of golden antlers hung above them.

Harry looked around, hardly able to believe this was where he'd be living. 'It's amazing,' he muttered to himself.

After exploring upstairs and taking his time to unpack, Harry sat alone on his bed, with a view out the window of the moonlit loch. He lay back, thinking over the events of the day. From the bizarre investiture ceremony, to the royal feast, to the strange pain he'd felt in his scar when he looked at Prince Philip, it was the weirdest and most tiring day of his life. But as he stared up at the sculpted, wooden canopy above him, he couldn't help but smile.

He was here, in the grandest school in the world, a member of a noble house and the royal family. It wasn't a dream anymore – it was real.

— CHAPTER EIGHT —

The Mixology Master

The first week at Balmoral passed in a whirlwind of peculiar lessons, bewildering passageways, and trying to get to grips with etiquette and protocol. As Harry and Beatrice navigated the castle, they couldn't help but marvel at how absurdly prestigious everything was.

Their lessons took them to all corners of the castle, and the challenge was not simply finding their way around, but avoiding the wrath of Michael Fawcett, the surly and untrustworthy caretaker. Every time they took a wrong turn and ended up near the forbidden East Wing or some other off-limits part of the castle, Fawcett was there, seemingly appearing out of thin air.

'What are you two doing here?' he would snap, glaring down at them suspiciously. 'This part of the castle is not for the likes of you.'

'We're sorry, we got lost,' Harry explained more than once, only to be met with a sneer.

'Lost, were you?' Fawcett repeated mockingly, leaning in closer. 'Or perhaps you were trying to find a shortcut back to your humble roots, eh? Spencer blood always has a way of straying, doesn't it?'

The murmurs from other students followed him around the castle, too. Everyone knew who he was, but while some were almost sycophantic and reverential, others showed a clear dislike for him, especially the Stuarts. When passing Stuart students in their silver and purple uniform, he would catch snippets of their whispers:

'That's him, you know, Spencer the usurper,' one girl said.

'Are you missing your council estate?' Will snorted as Harry passed, trying to keep his head down.

'What's next, letting the public in for tea?' sneered another.

'Ignore them,' Beatrice whispered fiercely when she noticed Harry's face fall. 'It's jealousy. They know that you are a Windzor, and they know that you're higher up in the line of succession than most of them.'

In exasperation Harry asked her, 'But then why are they being like this? I thought the whole point of this place is hierarchy and fawning to those higher up than you?'

'But that's the thing, Harry,' Beatrice reasoned. 'You have been out of the picture for so long, some people even thought you had died. And now suddenly you're back and second in line to the throne! You have no idea how insecure lots of these people are, especially the Stuarts,' she added with a scowl.

Unsure if to feel reassured or worried by this explanation, Harry shook his head wearily.

*

One evening, their lessons took them to the highest turret of the castle for Astrology. The stone floors were cold underfoot, and a chill hung in the air as they gathered around Professor Debbie Frank, who stood swathed in velvet robes, pointing to the constellations above.

'Now, pay attention,' she declared dramatically. 'The stars are the only true guide to a royal's destiny. This constellation here foretells success and prosperity for the Windzors this year, while this one suggests that the commoners will continue to adore you from afar.'

Harry glanced at Beatrice, who rolled her eyes discreetly. He only just about suppressed a laugh as they were then instructed to chart the stars that would help guide them to finding a royal suitor.

Apothecary classes took place in the Victorian greenhouses behind the castle. The air was thick with the scent of damp earth and herbs, and Princess Margaret, who taught the class, often arrived looking as though she'd freshly rolled out of bed, a lit cigarette dangling from her lips.

'Today, we'll learn about the various uses of poppies,' she said, her voice slightly slurred, as she held up a flower. 'Good for pain relief ... and for making an otherwise dreary evening duty a little more tolerable.'

The other students snickered, but Harry could only stare wide-eyed as they learnt about 'herbal remedies' that seemed to blur the line between medicinal and recreational.

'Is this ... legal?' he whispered to Beatrice.

'For us, or for the public?' she answered with a smirk.

The most excruciating lesson was History of Majesty, taught by Prince Edward, Duke of Kent, a dreary, old man who had a voice as dry as parchment. He droned on and on about royal lineage, the importance of the bloodline, and the many achievements of their forebears.

'You must remember,' he said gravely, 'that the royal line is not solely about power, but purity. Our blood is what makes us superior, but with poor choices, royal blood can become thin – and I'm not talking about haemophilia.'

Harry found himself sinking lower in his seat as the Duke of Kent spoke, painfully aware of the not-so-subtle glances sent his way.

'All of us here at Balmoral are connected,' he continued. Even those, like myself, who will never sit on the throne, have a duty to support those that will. As our sovereign shares our blood, it is not only the monarch that rules, but our family. I am first cousin to the Queen herself, but also second cousin and first cousin, once removed, to the sadly, departed Prince Charles ...'

'First *and* second cousin to my father?' Harry murmured to Beatrice. 'How does that work?'

Stifling a snort, Beatrice whispered back, 'No idea. I guess we are all cousins here, one way or another, it's best not to think about it too much.'

In Smarms, the class dedicated to mastering the art of charming the public and maintaining the illusion of superiority, they were taught by Mark Bolland, the royal PR guru. He strutted back and forth in front of the students, instructing them on how to project an aura of effortless nobility.

'It's all about the façade,' he said with a knowing leer. 'You must always appear gracious, even if you think the person before you is a complete waste of space. The trick is to smile while looking down on them; remind them you're superior but make them feel grateful for it.'

The students spent the class practicing their small talk and haughty expressions, and Harry couldn't help but feel uncomfortable. It felt so artificial, but he did his best, trying to imitate the effortless confidence that the others seemed to have. He wondered how the public didn't see through this, the leering and the condescending. But, he reasoned, this is what the lessons were all for. As Bolland constantly reminded them, 'Practice makes the plebs genuflect.'

One of the more surreal classes was Tax Fraud and Evasion, taught by Princess Anne in a wood-panelled study, with heavy, velvet curtains drawn against prying eyes. Anne was brisk and matter-of-fact as she outlined the ways the royal family maintained their wealth.

'Firstly, it is imperative that the public never know exactly how much we're worth,' she said, her voice sharp. 'Remember: the less they know, the more they'll be willing to give. And so today, we start with the most important of considerations – inheritance. When we die, not only do we pass down our titles, but we also pass down our wealth. The common people pay something called inheritance tax,' she said, wrinkling her nose. 'We, of course, do not. It does take a bit of effort to avoid though, and so I shall demonstrate how this can be done. As you will discover, to the well organised estate, dodging death duties is but the next great endeavour.'

Princess Anne paused, looking out over her class.

'I hope you are all taking notes.'

Harry quickly got out a notebook and began scribbling things down, half in disbelief that this was an actual lesson.

The class that Harry was most intrigued by was Deference Towards the Monarchs. Ever since he had briefly met Piers Morgan in the summer, something had been troubling him. He remembered the Queen Mother's remark about feeding the press and how Piers Morgan had seemed so fascinated by him at the Goring Hotel. Harry wondered if, beyond simply teaching, Morgan might have taken the job for his own, ulterior means.

He flinched as the door closed with a snap, and Piers Morgan walked to the front, scanning the students until his eyes rested on Harry.

'Welcome to Deference Towards the Monarchs,' he began, his voice slick with the self-assuredness of someone who knew the game all too well.

'In this lesson, we'll discuss how the media can be both your greatest ally and your worst enemy. You see, the press and the royals share a long, symbiotic relationship; sometimes we build you up, sometimes we tear you down. It's all about keeping the public's interest ... balanced, of course.'

With his fingertips on his desk, he leaned forwards, eyes glinting as he added, 'We know things about the royal family that never make it to print ... we leak just enough to keep people hooked, without bringing down the whole, fragile fantasy. Think of it as a little give and take, or, as you might learn, a bit of phone tapping, a well-timed paparazzi shot, or a headline to divert attention from certain bigger scandals.'

Harry felt a twinge of foreboding. There was something in Morgan's tone – an edge of menace. The man had been involved with the tabloids for years, and Harry couldn't shake the suspicion that people like Morgan may have played a darker role in the events that had torn his family apart.

As if sensing Harry's discomfort, Morgan looked at him.

'A case in point,' he said smoothly. 'Diana, Princess of Wales ... she was a master at working the media, but even she didn't always know where the line was. Sometimes the game catches up with you. It's a dangerous thing, being both a royal and a public darling.'

During a lingering pause, some students glanced at Harry whilst others looked away uncomfortably.

Morgan then began the class, displaying examples of headlines about royal scandals. Explaining how they were crafted and curated to perfect the balance between enticing and appeasing the public.

Harry half-heartedly took notes, but he was distracted and felt quite empty for the rest of the lesson.

*

The next morning, halfway through breakfast, Harry's swan, Odette, soared through the Ballroom's windows, landing gracefully on the Plantagenet table. Attached to her leg was a scroll sealed with the Queen Mother's insignia.

'It's for you,' Beatrice said, untying the note and passing it to Harry. Reading the neat handwriting, Harry saw that the Queen Mother had invited him to visit her cottage that evening.

Harry passed the note back to Beatrice with a smile, and said, 'At least that's something to look forward to after we get through Mixology with the Stuarts.'

A murmuring started rippling along the tables. Harry looked up and saw another bird flying towards them. Squinting against the sun, he couldn't quite make out what it was. But the way it flapped its wings looked ungainly – contrasting noticeably with the swans gliding down elegantly to the other tables.

A loud, crude honk drew mirth from the watching students

and Beatrice let out a horrified, 'Oh no!'

The bird landed with an undignified thud on the table in front of her, as more people joined in the laughter.

'That's a goose!' said Harry, bewildered.

'I know,' moaned Beatrice, as she hunched her shoulders in humiliation. 'That's Cassandra – she's my mum's.'

The goose flung a newspaper onto the table and then sidled up to a nearby swan – attempting to arch its neck sophisticatedly. The swan hissed and took off, leaving Cassandra with her head down, looking glum.

'Oh, right,' said Harry, biting his lip. He didn't want to join in with the other people laughing at Beatrice. He had never seen her so embarrassed.

'Go on – get out of here,' Beatrice said shamefully to Cassandra.

The goose gave a petulant honk and started running clumsily down the table, flapping its wings and knocking glasses and plates everywhere. As it reached the end of the table, it threw itself into the air, flying cumbersomely upwards, back to the window and out.

After a clash, as the last, spinning plate hit the floor, there was a stunned silence.

Then, Will called out, 'Is Fergie still waiting for her golden egg?'

Harry looked at Will with loathing, hearing Beatrice's sobs by his side as she buried her head in her arms. But Will looked straight back at him, with insufferable glee, as he deftly stroked the head of his own large, black swan that had just landed softly beside him.

As people slowly lost interest, turning back to their breakfasts, Harry tried to distract Beatrice from her embarrassment.

'What's this?' he asked flippantly, pointing at the name of the paper.

Beatrice took her hands from in front of her puffy eyes and

looked down.

'Oh, have you never had this paper before?' she said meekly.

'*The Daily Pageant*,' Harry read aloud. 'No, I can't say I have.'

Regaining some of her usual spirit, Beatrice picked up the paper and opened it up in front of them both.

'This, really, is what it's all about,' she explained. 'This is where our great achievements and duties are reported each day.'

'Err, why has Fergie sent you a copy then?' Harry asked, finally cracking a smile, unable to keep his amusement under control any longer.

After giving Harry a brief, unimpressed glance, Beatrice said, 'I'm not sure ...'

She rifled through a few pages and then stopped abruptly.

'Oh no, she doesn't think this article is about her, does she?' Beatrice said exasperatedly, showing it to Harry.

FERGIE HONOURED FOR TROPHY TRIUMPH
Manchester United manager receives knighthood from Princess Anne for services to the nation for his historic success.

Harry grimaced. 'It looks like it ...'

Beatrice slumped back forwards, resting her head in her hands.

Looking through the next few pages, Harry said, 'I can see why my uncle didn't bother to get this paper. Is anyone actually interested or impressed by this stuff – hang on.'

He stopped on a page towards the centre and showed a small story to Beatrice.

'Look at this,' he said curiously. 'Someone tried to rob Coutts; apparently a high security vault was broken into, but nothing was stolen.'

'So, why do you care?' Beatrice replied, not particularly interested.

'Because,' said Harry, lowering his voice. 'It happened on the same day that I was there with the Queen Mother. We went to one of their secret vaults and took out a big, strange object.'

Looking at Harry quizzically, Beatrice said, 'What object? What exactly were you and the Queen Mother picking up from Coutts?'

'I don't know, she wouldn't tell me what it was, just that it was a secret,' Harry continued. 'It was enormous though, like a massive, heavy block. We had to take it out of their on a wheelbarrow.'

'A wheelbarrow!' Beatrice remarked, now looking intrigued. 'Look here, it says the guards found an abandoned wheelbarrow on the scene ...'

Harry grabbed the newspaper and read the rest of the article.

'What the hell?' he said. 'Do you think they were after the same thing that we took?'

'Who knows,' Beatrice said. 'Come on though – we need to get moving or we'll be late to Mixology.'

Harry dropped the paper back down on the table with a lingering, troubled look, then followed Beatrice out of the Ballroom, and down the stairs to the lower part of the castle.

As they entered the cellar, a cool, damp ambience greeted them, and Harry noticed the rows of vintage wine bottles lining the walls. Prince Philip stood behind a wooden table, an assortment of spirits, mixers, and glassware arranged before him. He had an air of impatience about him and a menacing aura that quelled all chatter from the students as they took their seats.

'Today,' Philip stated, with a slow and profound intonation, 'we will be exploring the ancient art of Mixology – a skill that every royal must master. You may think this trivial, but it is far more than a matter of pouring liquids into a glass. The right cocktail can befuddle the mind, ensnare a suitor, or even –' his teeth glinted mischievously, 'smooth over an awkward diplomatic encounter.'

He scanned the room, as if daring anyone to chuckle at his jest. His eyes rested on Harry.

'Ah yes, Harry *Spencer*... our new royalty,' he said, raising an eyebrow. Will, sitting between Tom and Ed Lascelles, laughed sycophantically and Harry felt his blood rise to his cheeks, but remained silent.

'Tell me, Spencer, what do you get when you mix absinthe and champagne?'

Harry was at a loss, unable to answer.

'Death in the Afternoon,' Prince Philip chastised before, shaking his head disdainfully.

'Let's try another. Where would you find a Pisco Sour?'

Again, Harry had no idea and looked down at his desk, embarrassed.

'Peru, Spencer. The answer is Peru,' Philip sneered. He then turned around to look at the rows and rows of bottles behind him and ran an angular finger along them.

'Lastly,' Philip drawled, 'what is the difference between a Mojito and an El Draque?'

Harry remained silent once more, but then –

'A royal cares not for the schtick or the bubble, just pour me one quick and make it a double!'

The voice had come from Beatrice's bag and, spinning in his seat, Harry saw Beatrice mouth, 'Stabbers, no!'

Prince Philip whipped around; his face taught with wrath.

'How dare you speak to me in that tone,' he seethed.

'Please, sir,' protested Beatrice desperately, 'it wasn't Harry!'

'Well, who was it then?' he demanded, striding up to them.

Slowly and reluctantly, Beatrice lifted Stabbers out of her bag and put it on the desk. A few seconds passed that felt like an eternity as Philip glared down at the toy.

Then, shuddering back into life, it sang, 'To avoid the shame, one must pass the blame, for we never complain and never explain!'

Philip glowered down at it, then at Harry suspiciously, then back at Beatrice.

'I do not know what that *thing* is, and I do not want to know. *Never* bring it to my class again.'

Beatrice hurriedly put Stabbers back in her bag.

'As for my question,' Philip continued, in his usual drawl, 'there is no difference. Mojito and an El Draque are two names for the same drink.'

Philip swept back to the front, shaking his head, muttering to himself.

The class moved on to attempting a mythical drink, rumoured to be able to cure Windzor male pattern baldness. The recipe was complex, involving numerous ingredients and a precise shaking technique that no one seemed to master. Peter Phillips managed to spill half his concoction over the table, sending bits of mint and crushed ice flying in every direction. By the end of the lesson, no one had succeeded in creating the miracle cocktail, much to Philip's disappointment.

'Hopeless, the lot of you,' he muttered, before dismissing the group.

As they left the cellar, Harry couldn't shake the feeling of being singled out.

'Why does he hate me so much?' he muttered to Beatrice, who walked beside him.

'I don't think he hates you,' Beatrice said gently. 'You're ... different. He's always been a stickler for the rules and titles and ... well anyway, what does it matter if one senior royal doesn't like you, the Queen Mother is your biggest fan, isn't she?'

Later that day, Harry and Beatrice went to visit the Queen Mother at her Garden Cottage in a secluded corner of Balmoral estate, near the forest. It was a pretty, little house nestled among rose bushes, with ivy climbing up the stone walls.

'Ah, my dears,' she greeted them warmly, her eyes crinkling with age and kindness as she ushered them inside. 'I hope you have been doing the Plantagenets proud; how has your first week been?'

They sipped tea and chatted, telling her about their lessons. The topic of Tax Fraud and Evasion jogged Harry's memory about the newspaper article on the attempted Coutts robbery.

'I saw in the paper that there was a break-in at Coutts, Granny,' Harry said casually, though he watched her face carefully. 'It happened on the same day you and I were in London.'

The Queen Mother's expression tightened for a fraction of a second, but then she chuckled. 'Oh, I'm sure it was just some foolish criminal trying to make a name for himself. Nothing for us to worry about.'

'But the story mentioned something odd,' Harry pressed on. 'An abandoned wheelbarrow left at the scene. As if they were trying to take something ... large.'

There was a pause, one long enough for Harry to sense her agitation.

'People always leave such odd details in these stories,' she said dismissively. 'Newspapers are notorious for getting things wrong – surely you've learnt that in your Deference Towards the Monarchs lessons?'

After an awkward silence, Beatrice changed the subject, and the Queen Mother seemed relieved. They spent another hour there chatting, as the sun slowly edged lower towards the forest.

As they made their way back to the castle, Harry was thinking about the newspaper story again, and the Queen Mother's evasive answers. The vault. The wheelbarrow. The attempted robbery. It all had to mean something. He thought once again about the mysterious object that he and the Queen Mother had withdrawn from that vault.

'What if the date isn't a coincidence?' Harry said to Beatrice as they climbed the steps to the castle entrance. 'What if they had been trying to steal the same thing that the Queen Mother and I had taken earlier that day?'

'Then maybe you were lucky and got it just in time,' Beatrice replied. 'Maybe she knew someone was after it?'

'Maybe,' Harry agreed. 'I wonder what that object was.' He fell silent as they got to the door. He felt a prickle on the back of his neck and a slight sense of disquiet as he looked up at the countless windows of Balmoral, the last rays of evening sun reflecting off them like a hundred, amber, roving eyes.

— CHAPTER NINE —

The Gentleman's Duel

Harry was starting to find his footing at the castle, but Will's constant jibes were making it more difficult. Will seemed to delight in needling Harry every chance he got, pointing out any small mistake or misstep, making snide remarks about his lack of royal upbringing. It was becoming harder to brush off, and Harry was finding it increasingly taxing to keep his temper in check. One morning at breakfast, Harry glanced over the weekly timetable pinned up on the wall and felt his stomach drop.

'Great,' he grumbled, seeing that they would have shooting lessons with the Stuarts later that week.

Beatrice shrugged and said optimistically, 'You'll do fine.'

'Yeah, maybe,' Harry said, feeling a knot of anxiety form in his stomach. 'I've never really had the chance to shoot that much, and if I'm useless at it, Will is going to be insufferable.'

Beatrice looked at him sympathetically. 'Don't worry, it's not that difficult really. You'll quickly get the hang of it.'

As they were talking, an elegant swan glided across the Ballroom. It stopped in front of Peter and carefully dropped a small ball on the table in front of him.

'What's that?' Harry asked, watching as Peter picked it up.

'It's my Court Circular Ball,' Peter explained, turning the small, shining orb over in his hand. 'It tells me all the royal duties and engagements scheduled for today. My mother ordered one for me, to remind me, since I'm a bit forgetful.'

He looked up at the top table and saw Princess Anne smiling at him encouragingly. Harry raised an eyebrow, impressed by the intricate design.

'So, it tells you everything you're supposed to be doing?'

'Exactly. It's to get me used to checking it, so I don't forget my duties when I'm older.'

Just then, Will sauntered past, whispering to Tom and Ed. But, catching sight of the ball, he snatched it from Peter's hand, holding it out of reach with a mocking grin.

'Oh, don't worry, Peter, you probably won't have much to do anyway. Maybe the odd opening ceremony at a public swimming pool, if you're lucky.'

Peter stood up crossly, trying to grab the ball back.

'Honestly,' Will continued, ignoring Peter's protests, 'why bother checking it every day anyway? Most of the time, there's barely anything on it. When I'm king, I'll make sure to do as little as possible. I bet the public wouldn't even notice if we used body doubles or kept recycling the same old photos.'

Noticing the argument from the staff table, Princess Anne got up and hurried towards them, fixing Will with a steely glare.

'And what do you think you're doing, Will?' she demanded. 'If you think you'll be able to slack off when you're king, you are sadly mistaken.'

Will rolled his eyes. 'Oh please, Aunt Anne. It's not as if you've done that much this year, yourself.'

'Oh really?' Anne retorted, crossing her arms. 'I've officially opened three village halls, judged a county flower show, and cut the ribbon at a new bus station during these last six months alone. The papers don't call me "the hardest-working royal" for nothing!'

She took the Court Circular Ball from Will and handed it back to Peter with an encouraging smile. 'Be careful not to lose this, Peter. Those duties have your name on it in no time, I'm sure.'

With that, she bustled out of the hall, leaving Will scowling after her. Harry heard him muttering as he slouched away, 'Duty, what a meaningless word. Princess Margaret has it right – when I'm king, it'll be duty-free for me.'

*

Later that week, Harry, Beatrice and the rest of the Plantagenets went out to the shooting range, their breath misting in the crisp, morning air. The Stuarts were already there, including Will, who leant casually against a wall.

The instructor, none other than Prince Philip, surveyed the group with an air of impatience. His face, weathered from years of shooting and hunting, was stern as he handed out old but expensive shotguns.

'Mixology is one vital skill for a royal, but nothing compares to our need to shoot and to hunt,' he declared. 'Hunting and drinking go together – but do try to do most of the drinking after the hunt,' he said dryly. 'Careful with these, these are not toys. They've been in the family for generations.'

Harry eyed the shotgun he was given, its polished barrel feeling heavy and foreign in his hands. Prince Philip got out the targets: crudely drawn pictures of rare British animals like wild boar, weasels, and otters, pinning them up a distance away.

As Harry studied the targets, a knot formed in his stomach.

'Isn't that illegal?' he said fretfully to Beatrice, who was tinkering with her own shotgun. Prince Philip overheard and let out a bay of laughter.

'Illegal? Maybe for some, but the police have to ask the Queen's permission to even come onto the estate. And do you know what that means? No one ever gets permission ...'

Harry wasn't sure if Prince Philip was joking or not, but there was something chilling in the way he dismissed the law like it was nothing.

Peter was the first to step up for a turn at the range. He tried to hold the shotgun confidently, but he wasn't prepared for the kickback as he pulled the trigger. Peter dropped it in surprise, and the subsequent shot fired wildly, grazing his toe. He yelped in pain, hopping on one foot while the rest of the students gasped or stifled shocked laughter.

'Bloody hell,' Philip groaned. 'Everyone put down your guns, now! Don't touch them until I get back!'

He huffed as he helped Peter limp towards the castle, muttering, 'Blasted Phillipses, should stick to pony riding.'

As soon as Prince Philip was out of sight, everyone started talking excitedly. Will, always eager to show off, spotted a small object half-buried in the mud nearby. It was Peter's Court Circular Ball. Will picked it up, tossing it between his hands – the sun glinting off it as it rose and fell.

'Give it here, Will,' Harry said tersely.

'Giving orders now are we, Spencer?' Will taunted. 'Remember who you are talking to, little brother.' The other Stuarts laughed mockingly.

'Give me that ball,' Harry said more calmly, knowing Will was trying to provoke him.

'No, I don't think I shall,' Will dismissed. 'How about you win it back? Let's find out who's the better marksman. If you beat me, the ball is yours.'

It wasn't much, but it was enough to ignite the unspoken rivalry between them. Harry picked up the gun off the ground, took a step towards Will and looked at him cooly.

'Fine, let's go.'

Will grinned, giving Tom a handful of pinecones to throw into the air. Harry watched as Will quickly aimed his gun and shot them down, one by one, with practiced ease. The Stuarts applauded and clapped Will on the back.

'My turn,' Harry said, taking a deep breath.

Will threw the pinecones higher, but Harry instinctively traced his shotgun and fired with perfect precision. He hit every target, the crack of the shots echoing across the range.

The Plantagenets, watching closely, were stunned into impressed silence. Then, in a flash, Will tossed the Court

Circular Ball high into the sky. Without thinking, Harry reacted, pulling the trigger. The shot rang out, and the orb shattered midair, pieces of it scattering like dust. Harry's heart sank as the sudden ringing silence was only disturbed by the tinkling of glass shards hitting the floor. He hadn't meant to shoot it, but it was too late now.

Princess Anne, who had been watching from afar, stormed towards the group with an astonished expression on her face.

'Harry!' she barked, making everyone jump. She grabbed him by the shoulder and marched him away from the range.

'Come with me. There is something that I need to do ...'

Harry's blood ran cold as he was hauled off, sure that he was about to be expelled, wiped from the line of succession, and sent back to live with the Spencers, forever. Inside, Princess Anne continued to steer Harry through corridors, her hand like a vice on his shoulder. Stopping outside a classroom, Princess Anne knocked and entered.

'Please excuse my intrusion, professor, but could I please borrow Benjamin for a moment?'

Harry waited out in the corridor, unsure of what was going to happen to him. He looked left and right, half contemplating running for it, but then Princess Anne came back out of the classroom, joined by an older Plantagenet student.

'Harry,' Princess Anne said seriously, 'this is Benjamin Lascelles. He's our house Gamekeeper, leading the Plantagenet hunt competitions. You've shown a natural gift today, and that cannot go to waste. I want you to be our new Stalker.'

She placed her hand back on his shoulder, her earlier severity now replaced by something like pride. 'We'll make sure you're equipped with the finest gun.'

Harry blinked in surprise. Instead of punishment, he was being given an important role in his house! He looked at her, still unsure what to say, but feeling a surge of relief and pride.

After heading back to the Ballroom for lunch, Harry found

The Gentleman's Duel

Beatrice and explained everything that had happened.

'But you have to keep it a secret,' he said. 'No one can know yet.'

As if on cue, two older Plantagenets, Fred and Gabs Kent, sauntered over and quietly congratulated him.

'Welcome to the team, Harry,' Fred said, slapping him on the back. 'We're in the hunting party too. We'll see you at training but just wanted to say congrats.'

Harry smiled and thanked them both, but as they walked away, Harry saw Will and his cronies approaching.

'Thought you'd have lost your titles by now,' Will sneered.

Harry, feeling more confident after his conversation with Princess Anne, responded defiantly, 'Sorry to disappoint, but I'm not going anywhere.'

'Fine,' Will said coldly. 'How about we settle this once and for all – a gentleman's duel. Midnight, in the trophy hunting room. Are you in?'

Harry hesitated for a moment – Zara had overheard the challenge and shot him a warning look.

'You two need to stop this. Breaking rules won't do anyone any good, especially not you, Harry,' she warned.

But Harry, despite knowing that Zara was probably right, knew he couldn't back down now. 'I'll be there.'

'I'll be Harry's second,' interjected Beatrice, looking stubbornly from Zara to Will.

With an arrogant laugh, Will said, 'Even better. Well, until later ... come on, Tom, Ed.'

Will walked away, followed by the other two.

'What are you thinking, Harry,' Zara admonished. 'Don't you think you've got away with enough today?'

Not quite meeting her eye, Harry said stubbornly, 'It's not your problem.' He shifted in his chair to face away from her.

Zara got up in a huff. 'I'm telling you; this is stupid. Not everything is about you and Will, you know.'

She stormed away, leaving Harry feeling a bit foolish.

'Er, Bea, what exactly is a gentleman's duel?'

'Well,' Beatrice said, 'you know our sceptres – they aren't just for show ...'

'Wait, what do you mean?' Harry questioned, unsure if she was teasing him. He pulled out his sceptre from his pocket and thudded it against his palm and then looked up at Beatrice.

'Now you're getting it,' she said. 'Waving these around might appease the public, but against rival heirs – well, diamonds don't just look pretty, they are pretty hard.'

*

That night, Harry nervously glanced at the clock in the common room. It was 11.30pm, and Will's taunting words echoed in his head. He glanced over at Beatrice, who had just finished a game of Frock, Pauper, Sceptres with Fred Kent.

'You ready?' Beatrice asked quietly, as she joined Harry. He nodded, and the two of them quietly slipped nearer the door, trying not to draw attention to themselves.

As they went to open the door, a voice hissed from behind.

'Where do you think you're going?'

Zara was glaring at them, arms crossed.

'You're not seriously going to go through with this, are you?'

'Zara, we have to,' Harry insisted. 'If I back down now, Will will never let me live it down. Besides, I've got to stand up to him at some point.'

Beatrice nodded in agreement. 'It's about pride, Zara. You wouldn't understand.'

'Oh, I understand just fine,' Zara shot back. 'But you're being reckless. This whole duel thing is ridiculous.'

'Look, we are going. What are you going to do – follow us and try to annoy Will into submission?' Beatrice grumbled.

Zara pouted, clearly realising she wasn't going to talk them out of it. 'I'll do what I need to do. I can't stop you going and you can't stop me coming with you.'

After looking at Zara incredulously, Harry yanked open the

door and stepped over the threshold. Peter was curled up outside the entrance, snoring softly.

'Peter?' Harry whispered, shaking his shoulder. 'What are you doing out here?'

Peter yawned and rubbed his eyes groggily.

'I was looking for Tarquin after dinner, and so I thought I'd wait here, in case he came back – but I must have fallen asleep.'

'Who the bloody hell is Tarquin?' asked Beatrice impatiently.

'It's his stupid tortoise,' Zara said with an exasperated sigh. 'Come on, follow us, you can look for him along the way – as long as you're quiet. We've got somewhere we need to be.'

Peter blinked sleepily. 'Where are we going?'

'To the trophy hunting room,' Harry said, irritably. 'But if you come with us, you have to promise to be quiet.'

Peter agreed, and the four of them crept through the castle, the torches flickering on the walls as they passed.

They took a few wrong turns before finally reaching their destination. The room's door was slightly ajar. Harry pushed it and they stepped inside, at once awestruck by the displays. Mounted animal heads of innumerable species lined the walls, their glass eyes staring down at them. There were heads of antelopes with horns of all shapes and sizes covering every inch of the walls, and an enormous rhino head mounted above an empty fireplace, its immense horn curving up to the ceiling. In the centre of the room stood a tiger, caught in a frozen snarl. A large brass plaque beneath it read: *Shot by Prince Philip, India, 1961.*

'Blimey,' Beatrice whispered, turning in a slow circle to take in the entire collection. '1961 ... that's the same year that he became the first president of the WWF, when it was first founded. I wonder if they knew about this?'

'Look at this,' Harry said, ignoring her comments and pointing at a medal in a glass cabinet.

Beatrice walked over to Harry and gasped.

'I didn't know your father was the Plantagenet Stalker when he was here!'

'Neither did I,' he said quietly. It still resonated with Harry whenever he saw Prince Charles' name or portrait around the castle. Proof, if he needed it, that his father had been here, and that he was retracing those footsteps.

Beatrice, still examining the cabinet, said, 'It says here that Prince Charles and Prince Philip shot over fifty wild boar between them in one day, on a trip to Germany. Shooting is definitely in your blood, Harry.'

Zara, however, was staring at the door on the other side of the room.

'Where is Will?' she said urgently. 'Surely he should be here by now –'

She stopped mid-sentence, holding up her hand. Harry strained to listen and then heard it – a faint, shuffling sound coming from the corridor outside. He crept to the door and peeked through the crack and froze.

It was the caretaker – Fawcett, holding an old lantern that flickered, casting long, grasping shadows. He was muttering to himself, 'I know they're around here somewhere. I'll catch those little protocol-breakers tonight, just you wait ...'

Turning back to the others, Harry began to motion that they needed to retreat, but then –

'One must never be caught, one must never confess, an alibi you'll need at Pizza Express!'

Stabbers had activated in Beatrice's bag and was whirring and jerking, the shrill echo of its call bouncing away down the corridor.

'Who's there!' Fawcett called, and the light from his lantern grew brighter as he hurried towards the noise.

Panicking, Harry and the others darted to the door that they had come in from, rushed through it and down the passageway – desperate to get away. They came suddenly to a dead end and stopped to catch their breath, alert for any sound of pursuit.

'It must have been a setup; Fawcett was waiting for you!' Zara whispered angrily between gasps. 'I told you –'

'Shh,' Harry hissed, as he peered back down the passageway. 'He's coming!'

Harry turned and hurriedly approached a large door in the shadows and tried the handle.

'It's locked!' he exclaimed in desperation. Beatrice pushed him out of the way, and using her hairpin, she skilfully unpicked the lock and opened the door so they could scurry inside.

They waited, breathless, hoping Fawcett wouldn't find them. After a few nerve-wracking seconds, the sound of his footsteps faded, and Harry let out a relieved sigh.

'That was close,' he muttered. 'Too close.'

'Where are we now?' Beatrice asked, looking around the unfamiliar room. But before Harry could answer, a low growling filled the air.

Out of the shadows, beneath a looming bookcase, were three small but ferocious corgis, teeth bared, eyes glistening. They stood in a neat row; their hackles raised and began to advance slowly towards the intruders.

'Oh no,' Zara whimpered. 'I've read about these. They're the royal guard dogs. They're trained to protect the most valuable –'

'Whatever it is they're protecting, it's not worth getting bitten over!' Beatrice interrupted. 'Back out, back out!'

The four of them edged backwards, but one of the corgis lunged, and children bolted, throwing the door open and sprinting down the corridor. They didn't stop running until they reached the entrance to their common room, panting and out of breath.

'They could have killed us!' Peter moaned.

'Well, it's over now,' Zara said, trying to catch her breath. 'But what were they even doing there? Why would there be guard dogs in an abandoned room?'

'Do you realise where that room was though – it was in the forbidden East Wing,' Harry said, still wheezing. 'And did you see what they were standing in front of? That didn't look like a normal bookcase.'

Beatrice frowned. 'You're right. I've seen similar bookcases in our other castles, they almost always conceal a secret entrance.'

'What could be so important that they'd need the corgis to guard it?' Peter wondered aloud.

Harry exchanged a look with Beatrice, his mind drifting back to that newspaper article about the Coutts break-in and what Harry and the Queen Mother had taken from the vault.

'Whatever it is, it's something they don't want anyone to find,' said Zara dismissively. 'Now, if you don't mind, I want to go to bed before anyone comes up with another stupid idea to get us all killed, or worse, exiled.'

With a final, angry sniff, she went into the common room, meekly followed by Peter, leaving Beatrice and Harry to frown at each other in the gloom.

'Beatrice,' Harry said in a tired voice, 'how about next time we explore the castle at night, you leave Stabbers in your dormitory?'

As they headed through the common room and to their bedrooms, neither spoke. A minute later Harry climbed into his four-poster bed and stared blankly up at its roof. He lay like that for a while, eyes open, thinking about the dogs, the bookcase and what it could mean, until he finally drifted into a troubled sleep.

— CHAPTER TEN —

Samhain

The next morning, Harry and Beatrice sat in the Ballroom for breakfast, now looking back at their adventure the night before with relish.

'I have to admit,' Harry said, grinning, 'that was pretty fun. I mean, apart from nearly getting mauled by corgis.'

Beatrice agreed, her eyes sparkling. 'I wonder what they were guarding. There must be something behind that bookcase.'

Peter, who was sitting nearby, let out an exasperated sigh. 'Whatever it is, I want nothing to do with it.'

Zara put down her fork with a scowl. 'Honestly, you two are going to get yourselves involved in a scandal before you've even finished your first year here. Just leave it alone.'

Harry rolled his eyes, exchanging a smirk with Beatrice. From the far corner of the room, he saw Will staring at him with an unpleasant expression, one of both disbelief and resentment.

As they continued eating, a sudden flurry of wings drew their attention. Everyone turned to see a pearly white swan soaring gracefully down from the high windows. It landed lightly, right in front of Harry, holding a long, thin package wrapped in thick, waxed paper. A murmur of curiosity spread through the room. Harry picked up the attached note to read it.

DO NOT OPEN AT THE TABLE.
It's your new gun. It's a Purdey, so do not let others
see it before the hunt, or everyone will want one.
Meet Benjamin at the Glas-allt-Shiel hunting
lodge this evening for training.

Princess Anne

'That's the royal hunting lodge,' Beatrice whispered, looking over Harry's shoulder. 'That's normally reserved for the most special shooting weekends.'

Harry's heart skipped a beat with excitement, but before he could say anything, Will swaggered over from the Stuart table, staring at the package.

'What's this, Spencer? A present?' He reached out, feeling the shape through the paper. 'It's a gun, isn't it?' His tone was incredulous. 'First-years aren't supposed to have their own weapons. You're not allowed to be part of the hunts!'

Beatrice, unable to resist winding Will up, smirked. 'Oh, it's not just any gun, Will. It's a Purdey – top of the line.'

Will's eyes darkened with jealousy. 'How would you know about that brand?' he sneered at Beatrice. 'Your mother couldn't afford one of those even if she sold royal access to dodgy businessmen again.'

'Come on, Bea,' Harry said, nudging her gently. 'Let's go.'

They left the Ballroom together, heading to a quiet courtyard to open the package properly, before their first lesson.

The day seemed to drag as Harry's excitement grew. Although he had never really enjoyed the shooting weekends that he had been on occasionally, he was starting to understand the lure of rural sports and, unlike when living with Spencers, he now didn't have to be self-conscious about his talent. He could hardly concentrate in his lessons, impatiently watching the clock until it was finally time to head out for his training.

As he approached the Glas-allt-Shiel lodge, Harry took in

the beauty of the view. The pine forest covered the hills that sheltered this part of the estate. The landscape felt both wild, and yet ordered, with the hunting lodge nestled in a corner of the forest, looking as if it had always been there. Smoke curled lazily from the chimney, and several magnificent horses were tethered outside.

Benjamin was waiting, leaning patiently against the lodge's wall. He gave Harry an appraising look, his eyes then resting on the gleaming gun nestled on his shoulder.

'Now, Princess Anne has vouched for your shooting ability, but there is a lot more to a hunt than just the final kill,' Benjamin began. 'You've got to know the rules of the hunt, and, from what I've heard, you haven't had that much experience in this sport.'

Harry simply nodded, listening attentively.

'The hunting party consists of seven people,' Benjamin explained, ticking them off on his fingers. 'First, we have the three Gunners, they're our primary shooters, aiming for as many quail as they can find. Each quail is worth 10 points for our party.'

He pointed to a couple of distant figures practicing on the far side of the field. 'Those are the Baiters. They flush badgers out of their setts and towards the opposing Gunners, making their job a lot more difficult. It's all about strategy and interference.'

Harry raised an eyebrow. 'Seems a bit chaotic,' he remarked.

Benjamin chuckled. 'Oh, believe me, it is. And then there's the Gamekeeper – that's me. I help prepare the grounds for each event, ensuring that there are no unwanted pests around to interfere. And on the day, I'm the one who registers all the birds shot by our Gunners. They bring them back to me, and I count the points.'

'And what about me?' Harry asked, eager but with a trace of trepidation. Benjamin's expression grew more serious.

'You're the Stalker, the most important hunter in the party.

Your job is to find and shoot the trophy kill of the event. For each hunt, a different animal is chosen, and the first Stalker to take it down wins 100 points. Usually, whoever bags the trophy kill, ends up winning the entire hunt.'

Harry's eagerness subsided. 'What animal would that be though?' He swallowed, feeling a knot form in his stomach. 'I mean, I like target practice, but I've never really ...' He trailed off, unsure of how to express his reluctance.

Benjamin looked at him curiously. 'You have shot animals before, surely?'

'Well,' Harry said, hesitating, 'I've been on shooting weekends and ... no, to be honest. I've never shot an animal, only targets.'

A frown crept onto Benjamin's face. 'Ah, I see. Well, I'm sorry to hear that – you've missed out. But I'm sure you'll be a natural at it, like your father and grandfather.'

Despite his encouragement, Harry felt uneasy. He wanted to prove himself and live up to his father's reputation. But, as he remembered the trophy hunting room, his mouth went dry. Would he want to see his name on a plaque below a tiger or another magnificent creature?

But Benjamin quickly shifted gears, clearly sensing his doubts. 'For now, let's focus on your aim,' he said briskly. He handed him some ammo and gestured at the cages he'd set up in the field. 'We'll start with something simple; these are hardly animals anyway. It's simply target practice with a few more feathers.'

For the next hour, Harry practiced shooting at various birds as they were released from the cages by Benjamin: magpies, jackdaws, wood pigeons. He hit most of them, though he winced every time a bird fell from the sky.

Benjamin watched closely, offering tips and corrections, and as the sun dipped below the horizon, he finally looked satisfied. 'You've got good instincts,' he said. 'Just need a bit more confidence.'

As they returned to the castle in the fading light, Harry couldn't shake his mixed feelings. He was proud of how quickly he was learning, and part of him was excited to be a part of the hunt party – to prove that he belonged. But the idea of shooting the trophy animal, whatever it may be, weighed heavily on him. He couldn't help but wonder: was this really what he wanted to be a part of?

'See you later, Harry,' Benjamin said, giving him a slight wave before heading off to the library.

'Yeah, see you,' Harry replied distractedly. When he entered the common room, Beatrice was waiting for him, impatient to hear about his first practice session.

'Well?' she asked, anxiously. 'How was it?'

Harry managed a smile. 'It was ... interesting,' he said. For now, he decided, that was something he'd have to think about on his own.

*

It was Samhain, and the castle was festooned with a truly bizarre array of decorations. Instead of plastic bats and cobwebs, the corridors and halls were lined with real, preserved animals; exotic species from all over the world, each more grotesque than the last. Vampire bats hung from the chandeliers; their wings frozen in macabre poses. A giant flying fox, its leathery wings stretched to full span, was mounted on the wall of the entrance hall, and smaller, odd-looking creatures peered down from every corner. The usual house banners had been replaced with pelts and stuffed specimens, giving the entire castle a strange, gothic atmosphere. Harry found the display unsettling, but he was getting used to the strange ways of the school.

As he and Beatrice made their way to Smarms class, they wondered what the lesson would entail. They both found the lessons quite fun but were not particularly keen on the professor. As usual, Professor Bolland had taken up his spot, perching on his desk at the front. Today, however, he seemed particularly enthused.

'Right, my little lordlings and ladies,' he announced with a flourish, 'today we're moving on to something absolutely essential in your royal toolkit: how to make the public adore and bow before you.'

He paused dramatically.

'Today, we shall master ... the royal wave.'

The students glanced at each other in excitement.

'Pair up!' Professor Bolland commanded. 'We'll be working on the swirl and twirl technique.'

Beatrice found herself paired with Zara, who approached the task with a determination bordering on obsessive. Bolland held up his hand and demonstrated the movement.

'Swirl and twirl, swirl and twirl,' he intoned, as his wrist moved in a delicate and practiced motion. 'You see,' he continued, 'you must give just the right amount of movement; too much, and you look inebriated, but too little, and you look disinterested. Royalty is about finding the perfect balance between indifference and a mere hint of graciousness.'

Harry recalled with a surprised revelation, the exaggerated wave that had got him in so much trouble with his Uncle Spencer last year. What Professor Bolland was demonstrating in front of the class, looked inexplicably alike the wave that Harry thought he had invented. He remembered what the Queen Mother had said to him, that night at Tarrystone, 'It's in your blood ...'

Beatrice attempted her own wave, but Zara rolled her eyes in distain.

'No, no, no,' Zara said sharply. 'It's not that hard, Bea. Honestly, you look like you're swatting a fly. You need to put your wrist into it, but not your whole arm. It's swirl and twirl, not flap and flop!'

Harry couldn't help but chortle, but Beatrice shot him a sour look.

'Maybe it's not as easy as you make it out to be, Zara,' she muttered through gritted teeth.

After a few more minutes of choruses of 'swirl and twirl', Professor Bolland continued his lecture.

'That's a good start, but you must all practice the wave for homework. Now however, it's time for the second most important skill for any royal: the meet-and-greet.'

The students gaped at him, wide-eyed with horror.

'Yes, yes, I know,' Bolland said with a titter. 'Interacting with the public can be terribly unpleasant. But rest assured, you will only be mingling with the "cream of the crop" – those who have been given titles and awards so that they actual feel like they deserve to meet us, silly things. And, fortunately, the only phrase you truly need to know is: *and what do you do?*'

He repeated it, loudly and precisely, with his nose raised, bottom lip stuck out and eyes half closed.

'You must drawl it out, give it an air of complete disinterest! Royalty does not ask questions because it cares, but because it's expected to.'

Bolland made them carry on in their pairs, wandering around the classroom to observe them.

Beatrice took a deep breath and projected, 'And what do you *doooo*?'

Zara shook her head impatiently. 'No, Bea! You're trying too hard. You have to sound like you couldn't care less! It's: and what do *youuuu* do? Like you're so bored, you're about to fall asleep standing up.'

Beatrice clenched her fists, her temper wearing thin. 'It's ridiculous,' she snapped. 'Why would anyone even want to speak to us if we're going to be so rude?'

'Because that's how it's done,' Zara argued back. 'It's tradition, it's how things are supposed to be. It's how we remind them that we're better than them.'

'That's stupid,' Beatrice muttered under her breath.

At the end of class, Beatrice caught up with Harry, still fuming.

'I can't stand her,' she complained. 'I mean, she's acting like she's already on the rota, attending events. She'll be lucky to get a gig any better than opening a job centre. Then again, with how far down the line of succession she is, she might as well get in the queue.'

Harry heard a sob as Zara sped past them, her eyes brimming with tears. It was clear she'd overheard Beatrice.

'Zara, wait –' Harry called, but she didn't stop. She disappeared around the corner, leaving Harry and Beatrice standing there, feeling an uncomfortable sense of guilt settle over them.

'Great,' Beatrice muttered, crossing her arms. 'Now, she's upset.'

'Well, she was a bit insufferable in the lesson,' Harry offered, trying to be supportive. But he could see that Beatrice felt bad about what had happened. 'Maybe you should talk to her later?'

'Maybe,' she conceded, though she didn't look convinced.

Harry glanced back towards the direction Zara had gone.

'This is all so complicated,' he said. 'I thought learning to be a royal would be about titles and history, not ... well ... waving and making people feel awful.'

'Welcome to the world of aristocracy,' Beatrice replied dryly.

*

The Samhain feast was a sight to behold, a spectacle of game meats shaped into grotesque and ghoulish forms to match the macabre season. Plates overflowed with roasted partridge, venison ribs drenched in crimson sauce, and wild boar sausages carved to look like writhing serpents. There were black pudding pies shaped like bats, and pâté moulded into skulls, with grinning, bony smiles. The students gorged themselves, enchanted by the extravagance of it all. Harry and Beatrice sat together, marvelling at the delicious array before them, trying to decide what to try first.

As the feast was reaching its peak, the doors of the Ballroom were thrown open with a loud crash. Everyone turned in surprise to see Piers Morgan stumble in, petrified and out of breath.

'Bull!' he gasped. 'Bull, in the cellar! Thought one would like to know!'

He collapsed onto the floor in a heap.

Panic erupted in the hall as students jumped up from their benches, shouting and looking around frantically.

Harry heard horrified cries such as, 'Not the vintage wine!' and 'We need to save the sherry!'

The Queen stood, raising her sceptre, commanding immediate silence.

'Prefects,' she ordered sharply, 'escort your houses back to their common rooms. Immediately!'

In the chaos, Harry and Beatrice began to follow the rest of the Plantagenets, but something nagged at Harry's mind.

'Zara!' he whispered to Beatrice, tugging at her sleeve. 'She's not here, she won't know about the bull – we need to find her!'

'I think I know where she might be,' said Beatrice. 'I heard Gabs say she saw her crying in the billiard room earlier. That's not far from the stairs down to the cellar.'

Harry looked panicked. 'What if she's still there?'

Without another word, they ducked out of line, slipping through a side passageway as the prefects ushered everyone else away.

As they hurried through the windy passages, they caught sight of something strange. Prince Philip was moving swiftly and purposefully in the opposite direction to the other professors. He was muttering something under his breath, and there was a gleam of excitement in his eyes, like he was on the hunt.

'What's he doing?' Beatrice murmured, but Harry shook his head.

'Doesn't matter right now. We've got to find Zara.'

As they approached the billiard room, a pungent, earthy scent hit them, and they heard the unmistakable sound of something heavy, shuffling and snorting. Peeking around the corner, they saw it: a massive Highland bull, with shaggy fur and enormous, curved horns. It was just outside the doorway to the billiard room. It pawed the ground, snorting angrily, its eyes black and wild.

The door to the room was slightly open, and through the gap, they could hear a muffled whimper.

'Zara!' Harry uttered, his heart pounding.

The bull, sensing their presence, lumbered away, knocking the door fully open.

From their hiding spot, they saw Zara inside, pressed against the wall, her face pale with terror. The bull was blocking the only way out and it looked ready to charge.

'We have to help her,' Beatrice said urgently, but Harry had no idea what to do.

What could they possibly do against something so massive?

Then, a thought flashed through Harry's mind. It was ridiculous, absurd, but it was the only thing that came to him. Drawing on the lesson from earlier that day, he stood tall, puffing out his chest, and, with as much arrogance as he could muster, shouted, '*And what do youuuu do?*'

Beatrice stared at him, in disbelief. 'Are you out of your mind? It's a bull, not some pleb you can talk down to!'

But the bull had turned to face them, its eyes were bulging. It let out a loud, angry snort, and Harry knew he only had seconds before it charged.

'The wave!' he shouted to Beatrice, his bravery waning. 'We need to use the wave!'

Beatrice didn't hesitate. She positioned herself on the opposite side of the room to Harry, facing the bull. With an elaborate, exaggerated motion, she executed the most perfect royal wave, swirling her wrist precisely as Bolland had taught them. 'Swirl and twirl,' she whispered, and for a moment, it was as if the bull was entranced by the motion.

But then, it started to charge at her, its hooves thundering against the floor. At the last second, Beatrice dodged to the side, like a matador, and the bull stumbled, momentarily confused.

'Over here!' Harry shouted, catching its attention again, and he performed the wave as well, his wrist twisting and turning, swirling and twirling.

The bull spun and began charging towards him instead, and as it did, Harry felt a strange surge of adrenaline. He dodged to the side as Beatrice had, and the bull, unable to keep up with the rapid movements, started to sway on its feet, disoriented.

They kept this up – waving and dodging and chanting, '*And what do youuuu do*,' until the bull, utterly bewildered and dizzy, finally collapsed in a heap on the floor, panting heavily. The room fell silent, save for the bull's laboured breathing. Harry and Beatrice stood there, still in their ludicrous wave poses, not quite believing what they'd done.

A voice broke the silence.

'What in God's name is going on here?'

They turned to see Princess Anne, Prince Philip and Piers Morgan standing in the doorway, looking equal parts shocked and furious.

Harry opened his mouth to explain, but Anne cut him off.

'You two could have been killed! What were you thinking, facing down a bull like that?'

Harry stammered, not knowing what to say, but Zara stepped forwards, her voice shaky but determined.

'It was my fault, mummy' she confessed tearfully. 'I thought I could calm it down myself. I remembered what you taught me about calming down horses. But I couldn't, and then ... they saved me.' Her voice broke, and she wiped her eyes with her sleeve. 'Harry and Beatrice saved me.'

Anne's expression softened. 'You're lucky you weren't all

trampled. Zara, I'm taking ten points from you, for such recklessness.'

Zara looked down at her feet, ashamed.

'But,' Princess Anne continued, turning to Harry and Beatrice, 'I award ten points to each of you for bravery – and also, your quite flawless royal wave.'

As they were led back to the Plantagenet common room, Zara walked between Harry and Beatrice, her eyes still red but a small smile playing on her lips.

'Thank you,' she said quietly. 'I don't know what would've happened if you hadn't come.'

'That's what friends are for,' Harry said reassuringly, and Beatrice put her arm round her shoulders.

They reached the common room door, and for the first time since their arrival at the school, it felt like the three of them had truly formed a bond – a sense of camaraderie that went beyond titles and traditions.

— CHAPTER ELEVEN —

The Hunt

November brought with it a biting chill that seeped into every corner of the castle. Frost coated the windows each morning, and icy winds howled through the grounds, forcing most students to huddle inside the castle's thick, stone walls. Only the Queen Mother seemed immune to the weather, often seen pottering around outside, dressed in layers of tartan and tweed, tending to the grounds with the vigour of someone half her age.

Despite the cold, anticipation whirred through the school like electricity. The first big hunt of the season was drawing near, pitting the Plantagenets against the Stuarts in what was already being talked about as the showdown of the year.

The secret was out: Harry was the new Stalker for the Plantagenets, and now, wherever he went, students from all houses eyed him with either admiration or jealousy. The pressure was slowly getting to him, and he found it hard to sleep some nights, imagining the eyes of the entire castle on him as he sought out the trophy animal.

Thankfully, now that Zara was a firm friend, and was determined to get even since the bull incident, she had taken it upon herself to do everything to help him prepare. Under her guidance, Harry's tracking had improved, and he'd become more adept at navigating the wild landscape that surrounded the castle.

One afternoon, she handed him a faded and dusty book

titled *Trophy Hunting Through the Ages*.

'You need to know the history if you're going to be the best,' she said matter-of-factly.

Harry took the book gratefully, but what he found within its pages disturbed him. He read about the famous hunts of the Windzors and their ancestors – tales of aristocrats traveling far and wide to kill the rarest and most magnificent animals they could find. There was the story of Edward VIII, who, during an overseas trip to India, had shot not one but three Bengal tigers in a single day, before posing for photographs with their lifeless bodies. There was mention of George VI embarking on a safari in Kenya, where he killed black rhinoceroses and lions for sport, his trophies mounted in private collections and now collecting dust in forgotten estate halls.

Then there were the species closer to home, ones that had been hunted to extinction or driven to the brink in the British Isles. Beavers, once abundant in Britain, were wiped out by the 16th century due to relentless hunting for their pelts. Pine martens had become so rare that entire generations of people had never seen one in the wild. The pages detailing the fate of birds of prey were the most harrowing for Harry. Species like the red kite and the hen harrier had been all but eradicated in certain regions due to their being labelled as 'vermin'. The book didn't attempt to hide these facts, but it posed vague questions about how and why this had happened and, without a trace of irony, lamented that such loss had made the options for sport less 'interesting'.

One frosty afternoon, Harry, Beatrice and Zara stood by the frozen loch, the weak November sun casting a pale light over the glassy surface. Harry paused from reading the book, its grim contents swirled in his thoughts. He tried sharing some of the stories with Beatrice and Zara, but Beatrice shrugged.

'I suppose it's just how things were back then,' she said, only half-interested.

Zara was looking distractedly at the castle, her mind clearly elsewhere.

'It's not just "how things were", it's still going on,' Harry insisted, flipping to a page with an illustration of how best to poison hen harriers on grouse moors.

However, a strange sight caught their attention, abruptly halting their conversation. They saw a figure limping past them towards the castle. It was Prince Philip, his usually confident stride reduced to a painful shuffle.

When he noticed the trio, Philip's eyes seared into them.

'What are you three doing out here?' he questioned. He then saw the book in Harry's hands. 'What is this?'

Without waiting for an answer, Philip snatched the book from Harry. He glanced at the open page and his expression twisting into one of derision.

'Hen harriers,' he scoffed, shutting the book with a sharp clap. 'We don't want any of those pests around here.' He tucked the book under his arm and hobbled back towards the castle, leaving the three of them startled.

'He's even more bad tempered than usual,' Zara said.

'And what's up with that limp?' asked Harry.

Beatrice said, with a weak laugh, 'Maybe he's sampled one too many of his own concoctions ...'

*

Back in the warmth of the Plantagenet common room, they worked on their Smarms homework, though Harry was still thinking about his confiscated book. The assignment was painfully dull, writing congratulatory letters on behalf of the Queen to people who had turned one hundred years old.

'How many of these must she send out a year?' Beatrice wondered aloud, her quill scratching across the parchment.

Harry sighed, pushing his own letter away in frustration.

'No one actually thinks she's the one writing these, do they?' He leaned back in his chair, frowning. 'Anyway, I've had enough. I want my book back. I'm going to the staff room to get it.'

'Harry, you can't just –' Beatrice began, but he was already gone.

Harry wound his way through the castle, the chill of the stone walls making him shiver. When he reached the staff room door, he knocked but received no reply. He hesitated, then gently pushed the door open slightly, peering inside. What he saw made him freeze.

Prince Philip was sitting in a chair, his foot bare, and blood was oozing from a swollen, bruised big toe. The caretaker, Fawcett, knelt in front of him, cleaning the wound.

'I told you, sir, you need to be more careful. Those dogs –'

Philip interrupted him with a hiss of pain. 'I should have known that those mutts were badly trained,' he grumbled, wincing as Fawcett dabbed at the cut. 'I thought I'd get past them without issue, but those bloody corgis are vicious when they want to be.'

Harry stepped back, holding his breath, but the movement caught Philip's eye.

'You!' he barked. 'What are you doing here?'

Without thinking, Harry turned and ran – his footsteps echoing down the corridor as he sprinted back to the common room.

He burst inside, panting, and collapsed into a chair. Beatrice and Zara looked up, alarmed.

'What happened?' Beatrice asked.

'I saw Prince Philip,' Harry said breathlessly, 'and he was with Fawcett. His toe was all bloody and he said something about trying to get past the corgis!'

Zara's eyes widened. 'You mean ... the corgis guarding that bookcase?'

'Exactly,' Harry insisted. 'I think he was trying to get whatever they're protecting.'

'Do you reckon Philip had anything to do with the bull getting in during the feast?' Beatrice asked slowly. 'Remember we saw him heading in the direction of the East Wing when we were looking for Zara?'

Zara shook her head. 'No way, why would he have let a bull in, and where would he have got it from?'

But Harry was perturbed.

'I don't know,' he said. 'I think Philip's up to something though. Maybe he let it in as a distraction and then went to the room with the bookcase. Maybe that's when he got bit?'

The three of them sat in silence, the flickering fire casting shadows on the walls, as they tried to make sense of things.

*

The next morning arrived in a swirl of frigid mist and bright, cold sunlight. Harry lay awake in his bed at dawn, staring at the canopy above him, his insides twitching with anxiety. Today was the hunt, the day that had been looming over him like a storm cloud since he was handed the role of the Stalker. The pressure to win, to impress his peers, to uphold the legacy of his house – it all felt suffocating. And yet, underneath that pressure was something else, a quiet, gnawing dread about what he might have to do out there in the woods.

Down at the hunting lodge, the entire school seemed to have gathered, every student clad in their finest hunting attire – polished boots crunching on the frosty ground. The Plantagenet team, led by Benjamin, gathered around Harry, offering words of encouragement. Fred and Gabs, the two Badger Baiters, gave him confident pats on the back. Harry's gaze wandered to the other side of the clearing, where the Stuart hunting party stood huddled together, exchanging murmured words and glancing back at the Plantagenets.

Then came the sound of steps approaching and Harry looked up to see Prince Philip, flanked by Piers Morgan, striding towards the centre of the gathering. There was a crate on the ground, and Piers reached into it, handing out rifles to Philip, along with boxes of ammunition. When it was Harry's turn, Philip handed him his polished gun with a look that was somewhere between a sneer and a grimace.

'Here you go, a gun fit for a prince,' he said, his voice dripping with false encouragement. He tossed Harry an extra-large box of rounds, adding, 'You'll need every single one of these.'

The words felt like a challenge but Harry bit back a retort and took the rifle, feeling its weight settle heavily in his hands. He met Philip's eyes, seeing something unsettlingly sharp and calculating there, before Philip turned away, clapping his hands to signal that the hunt was about to begin.

'The trophy for today's hunt,' he announced loudly to the amassed crowd, 'is a red deer stag. Begin!'

Suddenly, everything sprang into motion. The Gunners from both parties scattered towards various parts of the clearing, rifles in hand, and for a moment the grounds were hushed with a tense, expectant silence. Harry stood rooted to the spot, feeling the cold seeping into his bones, before snapping out of it and moving towards the woods. He tried to block out the keen, hungry murmuring of the spectators and the pounding of his own heart, focusing instead on the weight of the gun against his shoulder and the crunch of the hard ground underfoot.

The calm was shattered when, somewhere behind him, a flock of quail exploded into the air, wings beating frantically, and gunfire erupted from all sides. The crack of rifles reverberated through the clearing, mingling with the shouts and baying of the crowd. Harry winced at the noise, feeling a knot tighten in his stomach. He had never quite understood the bloodlust that seemed to seize people during these hunts, and now, surrounded by it, he found it even more unpleasant.

Moving deeper into the woods, Harry spotted Fred crouched by a large, freshly turned hole in the bank, his breath clouding the air.

'Stand back, Harry,' Fred warned. 'There's a big one in here.'

The Hunt

Suddenly, a huge badger burst from the sett, its fur bristling, eyes wild with panic. It snarled and turned towards Harry, who stumbled back, raising his gun reflexively. But Fred intervened, waving his arms and shooing the badger away. The creature tore off through the brush, heading towards the Stuart Gunners.

'That'll cause some chaos,' Fred grinned, dusting off his hands. 'But you, Harry, you need to get deeper into the woods if you want to find that stag.'

Harry gave him the thumbs up and pressed onwards.

Harry could smell the scent of damp leaves and earth, and every sound seemed amplified in the stillness of the forest. Then, through the trees, he caught a glimpse of a large flank – smooth, grey-brown, and unmistakably deer-like. Exhilaration shot through him, although reluctantly he raised his rifle, only for Fred to appear again, shaking his head.

'That's a sika deer,' Fred murmured, disappointment evident in his voice. 'Keep going, deeper into the oak thicket.'

Harry kept going, and eventually, he found himself in a small clearing with the weak sun reaching through to the gnarled ground. And there, in front of him, stood the most magnificent creature he'd ever seen – a towering red deer stag, its antlers rising like a crown against the pale sky. It was old, its coat tinged with grey, and its eyes, large and deep brown, seemed to hold all the wisdom and weariness of the world.

Taking a deep breath, Harry raised his gun, trying to steady his hands. He looked down the cold, metal barrel at the animal, conflicted. He felt his throat tighten and his heartbeat pounding in his ears as he fought off his feeling of guilt. He had to do this, he told himself. He had no choice. And so, he fired.

But as he squeezed the trigger, something went wrong. The rifle jerked violently, the recoil slamming into his shoulder, and the weapon was wrenched from his hands, clattering to the ground.

The stag, startled, bolted into the trees, and Harry fell to his knees, shaking.

Picking up the rifle and reaching for the ammo box to reload, Harry noticed something peculiar. A small, oddly shaped piece of metal was lying on the ground, next to where the rifle had fallen. It didn't look at all like it should belong with the gun, and it had scorch marks that must have been caused by the misfire. Had Philip meddled with his gun, and was this thing what had caused it to malfunction? He picked it up, pocketed it and forced himself to continue, the sounds of the hunt echoing in the distance.

After nearly ten minutes, he stumbled upon the stag again, standing in the middle of a patch of sparse trees, panting heavily. It looked exhausted. As Harry watched, the stag's legs gave way beneath it, and it crumpled to the ground. This creature, once so noble and proud, was dying. He went tentatively closer but couldn't see a bullet wound.

Their eyes met, and Harry felt a jolt in his chest as if the stag were asking him for mercy, for kindness. He knew that leaving it like this would only prolong its suffering. Coarse and ragged breaths shook the animal's hide, the noise cutting right through Harry. Swallowing the lump in his throat, he stepped closer and, with shaking hands, raised his rifle.

He fired – the shot reverberating through the trees, and the stag's great head slumped back, the antlers cushioned by the fallen leaves of red and gold.

Silence followed – a heavy, suffocating silence that seemed to press down on him from all sides, then broken by rustling and approaching footsteps.

Prince Philip emerged from the trees, looking from Harry to the stag with an expression betraying his respect. After confirming the scores from each party's Gunners with Piers Morgan, he cleared his throat.

'The hunt is over and the Plantagenets have won!' he declared.

The crowd of people who had caught up, erupted in cheers, but Harry felt none of the pride or satisfaction that should have accompanied their victory. As he went to turn away, Philip caught his arm, a gleam in his eye.

'And now,' Prince Philip announced, 'the blooding!'

Harry seemed rooted to the spot as he watched Philip walk to the stag, drag a cloth through the wound, and upon returning to Harry, smear the blood over Harry's cheeks and forehead. The warmth and the smell made him feel sick, but to the smattering of applause, he forced a smile to the crowd.

As the crowd began to disperse, he wiped his face on his coat. He walked back to the hunting lodge, trailing behind the others, feeling numb. There, he handed over his gun and found Zara and Beatrice waiting, concern etched into their faces.

The Queen Mother appeared, taking in the dried blood on Harry's face and the way that he was cradling his hand.

'Are you injured?' she demanded. But without waiting for him to respond, she whisked him back to her cottage, insisting on tending to him.

Inside, as she cleaned and bandaged his hand, Harry told her about the rifle misfiring and showed her the metal piece that had come off his gun.

'I think Prince Philip did something to sabotage my rifle,' Harry said quietly. 'He handed it to me at the start of the hunt, I think he tampered with it.'

'Nonsense,' the Queen Mother said sceptically. 'Prince Philip would never sabotage one of his own. What would make you think that?'

'Because he's up to something,' Harry said guardedly. 'I saw him with an injured big toe, and I think I know what happened ... he was trying to get past the guard corgis in the forbidden East Wing.'

The Queen Mother's eyes widened in shock.

'How do you know about my corgis?' she demanded.

'Your corgis!' Harry exclaimed. 'What are they doing in the

castle? They nearly killed us!'

She pursed her lips, clearly debating with herself about what she should say.

'Those corgis are from the finest stock,' she said proudly. 'Years ago, when my daughter was only a teenager, I bought Susan for her – a darling of a corgi. It is from Susan that I've been breeding generations of the most perfect little sweethearts. My youngest are those three little rascals that you ran into.'

Her wistful expression turned back to one more serious.

'I must say, I don't know how you came across them, but if they gave you a scare, then it serves you right. They are highly trained for their job and the only people who need to know about them are Her Majesty and Laurens van der Post –'

She stopped abruptly, realising she had said too much.

'Who?' Beatrice asked.

'Enough,' the Queen Mother said hastily, shooing them out of her cottage. 'Mind your own business, children. Some secrets are best left alone, now out with you.'

As they walked back to the castle, Harry, Beatrice and Zara shared bewildered looks. They knew that whatever the Queen Mother's corgis were guarding, it must be very important.

Beatrice said determinedly, 'We need to work out what Philip is after.'

Zara nodded, 'Who was it that she mentioned?'

'Laurens van der Post,' answered Harry. 'I feel like I've heard that name before ...'

'Well let's find out who he is and I'm sure it'll lead us to whatever Philip is trying to steal.'

— CHAPTER TWELVE —

The Tapestry of Heirs-in-Thread

The snow fell in thick, soft flakes, turning the Balmoral estate into a picturesque, winter scene. Every tower was capped with white, and the sprawling grounds, usually lively with activity, had turned silent and serene. In the distance, the swans glided over the frozen loch, their necks wrapped in the turtleneck jumpers that the Queen Mother had knitted for them. Harry couldn't help but laugh when he first saw them, but the swans, used to such treatment, remained regal and unbothered by their festive attire.

Inside, preparations for Christmas had already begun in earnest. The Ballroom was being transformed into a vision of opulence, with enormous fir trees covered in twinkling lights, and garlands draped over every available surface. The tall fireplaces roared with warmth, chasing away the chill that crept through the stony corridors. Yet the castle couldn't escape the biting cold entirely.

As Harry wandered down a particularly drafty hallway, he overheard two professors muttering to each other, their breath misting in the icy air.

'Good old "Queen's Consent" again, I suspect,' one of them grumbled, pulling her shawl tighter around her shoulders. 'Blocked the Heat Networks Act before it even got to Parliament, didn't she? No underground heating or heat pumps for us, then,' she finished sarcastically.

The other professor let out a sigh and said, 'Yes, in retrospect, maybe that was a hasty decision by the Queen's lawyers. It is frightfully chilly, and I wouldn't say no to some twentieth-century heating. But, really, who do they think they are? Demanding that working-class people come onto our estate, to dig up our lawns and lay pipes everywhere, all in the name of sustainability.' The second professor ended the sentence with a sneer and such a melodramatic eyeroll that Harry wondered if they would be taught that in a future Smarms class.

He shook his head, half-listening. He knew enough by now to recognise that 'Queen's Consent' meant the royal family had, once again, used their influence to bend the rules to suit themselves, able to veto any law before it even got to be debated by MPs. As Harry carried on down the corridor, away from their irritable complaining, he wondered how many laws had been blocked or changed on a royal whim over the decades.

As the Christmas break was approaching, the topic of who was staying at Balmoral, and who was heading back to their family's estate, was on everyone's lips. As the students were not 'working royals' yet, they would not usually spend the holiday with the senior royals and the Queen at Balmoral. Even those students who needed to stay at the castle over the break, would not be enjoying the 'inner-circle festivities'.

From the rumours that Harry had heard about the debauchery and pranks that often took place, he was relieved to instead be looking forward to a bit of peace and quiet – especially avoiding Princess Margaret, if he could help it. He had heard enough stories about her approach to the Twelve Days of Christmas to keep a distance.

Will, naturally, took any opportunity to tease Harry about having to stay at Balmoral over Christmas.

'You know,' Will drawled, as they waited for the start of the next lesson, 'only spares with nowhere else to go, end up here over the holidays. How sad for you, Spencer.'

It was Beatrice who reacted first.

'Don't pretend you're happy about going home. Daddy only wants you there because you are next in line. It's got nothing to do with your charming personality.'

Will baulked, before retorting spitefully, 'But Uncle Andy does actually want me there, unlike *you*. Still homesick, are you, after being shipped off to live at Fergie's bedsit? I bet it's a relief to be staying here for Christmas, this year. One can only imagine the squalor and self-pity.' With a self-satisfied snigger, he pushed past them and into the classroom.

Harry cast a sympathetic look at Beatrice, who gave him a brief smile in return, though Harry saw a touch of sadness in it. It was true, she was staying at Balmoral too; she had received a letter from Fergie saying that the bailiffs were coming round again, so it would be better if she stayed away.

Harry was slowly realising that it wasn't just him who had a complicated family history. The announcement of Prince Andrew and Fergie's separation had been made public recently, but the arguments and negotiations of Beatrice, Eugenie and Will's living arrangements had been rumbling on for months. Although she wouldn't admit it, Beatrice had been saddened and unsettled by her father's abandonment of her, in favour of Will. And Will, too, had been deeply hurt by the upheaval and disruption. Beneath his uncaring demeanour, Harry was sure Will felt the absence of their parents just as much as he did. And now, he had even lost the affections of his adopted mother, Fergie. Although Will made jibes about Fergie, especially to Beatrice, Harry wondered if this was because he missed having her around and blamed her for the separation.

Harry still found it strange to think that Beatrice and Will had grown up together – they were so very different to each other. What was it that had resulted in Beatrice becoming

Harry's best friend, and Will, his bitter rival? Whatever it was, Harry would be grateful for some time without Will around.

As Harry and Beatrice made their way into the classroom and settled into their seats, Harry looked at the back of Will's head. Even now, Will was looking around restlessly, in need of attention. Harry, for the first time, felt something new when considering Will: pity.

Growing up a royal, Will had never lacked in luxury, or in getting his own way, but Will did also have insecurities. Being the next in line to the throne had made him arrogant and superior, but also extremely sensitive to embarrassment. Though he tried to hide it, Harry knew Will was bitterly disappointed to be spending Christmas at home; Prince Andrew was mired in yet another scandal and had been advised to lay low in the countryside, far away from the festivities at Balmoral. Harry wondered if Will's need to put other people down all the time was just his defence, when he was feeling vulnerable himself. Thinking about what he had heard about Andrew and Fergie and the seemingly endless scandal following that household, Harry appreciated the privacy that having been raised a Spencer had given him.

*

After their lessons, Harry, Beatrice, and Zara headed to the library, hoping for a moment's respite from the festive chaos to continue their search for information about Laurens van der Post. Ever since the Queen Mother had accidently mentioned that name, they had been going through countless books, hunting for a clue as to his identity.

They had been researching notable figures who had acted as mentors or advisors to the British royals but had come up empty-handed. They'd tried titles like *Friends in Your Highness Places*, *Fifty Shades of Men in Grey Suits* and *Royal Scandals for Dummies,* but Van der Post wasn't mentioned in any of them. It was as if he'd been deliberately erased, his presence in the royal circle scrubbed from history.

'It just doesn't make sense,' Zara muttered, as she pulled more books down from a shelf. 'If the corgis are guarding something for him and the Queen, he must be really important, but he's not mentioned anywhere.'

'Unless they're hiding something,' Harry said quietly. 'What if he has some kind of sordid past that they don't want anyone to find out about?'

Zara raised an eyebrow. 'You're suggesting a royal cover-up? The establishment would never allow that,' she said sarcastically.

Harry didn't laugh. Instead, his eyes drifted towards the far end of the library, where the entrance to the restricted Royal Family Archives was located. He'd seen it a few times, the heavy wooden door guarded by a brass plaque that declared it off-limits. Everyone apart from the senior royals needed special permission to access it. The thought of what skeletons and secrets lay within, both excited and perturbed Harry.

'What if the answers we're looking for are in there?' Harry asked, pointing towards the door.

Beatrice shook her head. 'Even if they are, we'd never be allowed in. Those archives are sealed tighter than a royal's will.'

'Maybe not if we had help,' Harry mused. And that was when he spotted a man approaching from the far side of the library. He was impeccably dressed in a tailored suit, his silver hair combed back with military precision.

'Good afternoon,' he said in clipped tones, his gaze flicking over Harry. 'You must be young Harry Windzor.'

'Uh, yes, sir,' Harry replied. 'And you are?'

'Sir Robert Fellowes,' the man answered snootily. 'I am Keeper of the Royal Archives. And, in case it matters to you, your uncle by marriage.'

Harry blinked. 'Everyone's related around here,' he muttered, not quite able to keep the sarcasm out of his voice.

Sir Robert continued to look straight at Harry.

'We are not in the business of jokes, Mr. Windzor. And I

will make myself perfectly clear, whatever you're looking for, you won't find it in *there*. The Royal Archives are not for prying eyes.'

'But —' Harry started, but Sir Robert held up a hand to silence him.

'Stay well away from that section of the library,' he warned. 'You are not authorised, and you will not be granted access. Do I make myself clear?'

'Yes, sir,' Harry said, gritting his teeth.

'Good.'

With a final, suspicious scowl, Sir Robert swept past them. As he rounded a bookshelf, Harry felt a surge of defiance rise within him. He had no intention of giving up. Whatever secrets Laurens van der Post held, and whatever role he'd played in the royal family's affairs, Harry was determined to uncover them, even if it meant going up against every tradition and rule that Balmoral stood for.

*

The morning sun filtered weakly through the icy windows of Balmoral Castle, its light glimmering off the snow that blanketed the estate. Zara had gone home for the holidays with her brother Peter, leaving Harry and Beatrice to explore the endless possibilities of festive activities on their own. And what better way to start, than with a game of Royal Monopoly?

Harry grinned as he pulled the lid off the ornate box, which was gilded in gold leaf and covered in crests of the royal family.

'Remember,' whispered Beatrice, 'Monopoly is officially banned here, so don't mention it in front of any senior royals.'

Curious, Harry asked why that was.

'Well, if there's anything that we royals are particularly good at, it's spending other people's money. My mum told me about one time she was playing the game with my dad, before, you know ... and as soon as they got the money out the box, it all descended into a sort of frenzy, with everyone trying to grab as much as they could. They didn't even get to the first turn.

Uncle Eddy was using the board as a shield to fend off daddy and his sceptre.'

Beatrice pulled out the playing pieces. Instead of the classic thimble, dog, or top hat, the pieces included a tiny replica of the crown, a corgi with a sparkling collar, and a tiny golden carriage. Harry chose the corgi, while Beatrice selected the golden carriage.

As they started to play, Harry noticed that the board was made up of different royal residences, starting with the modest Sandringham Estate, then Buckingham Palace, progressing to Balmoral, and finally to Windsor Castle, the most expensive property on the board. Instead of cards for Chance and Community Chest, there were decks for Privy Purse and Sovereign Grant.

'Who made this game?' Harry asked, rolling his eyes as Beatrice landed on Privy Purse and collected an enormous sum of money. 'I'm beginning to think it's a bit rigged.'

'Oh, it's just realistic,' Beatrice said airily, collecting yet another windfall as she landed on a tile labelled *Duchy of Lancaster, Untaxed Profits*. 'I mean, it's not like us royals actually pay taxes, after all.'

Harry was losing badly but then Beatrice landed on a space labelled *Go to the Tower*.

'Ha! Finally!' he cried, certain that this was his chance.

'Not so fast,' Beatrice said with a smirk, picking up a card she had collected earlier. She handed it to him and, crestfallen, he saw what was written on it: *Get Out of the Tower Free*.

Harry groaned and the game continued until Beatrice owned nearly every piece of prime royal real estate, and Harry's corgi was bankrupt.

The next morning, Harry woke up with a sense of excitement he hadn't felt in years. It was Christmas Day and there was a small pile of presents waiting for him at the foot of his bed.

The first gift was from the Spencers: a small leather-bound

journal with his initials embossed in gold. Harry saw they were *H.S.* and felt a bit of guilt tugging at him. Inside, there was a short, curt note. *We hope you are well. Take care.*

Harry sighed, with a mixture of appreciation and sadness. He remembered the last conversation he had had with his uncle when he was being dropped off at the train station. Some of his uncle's warnings now made more sense to him. He hadn't spared Althorp much thought during his time at Balmoral, but reflecting now, he realised how much that estate and the family meant to him. It had not been easy growing up there – an outsider but not understanding why – but knowing that they were there and thinking of him, gave him a sense of security that was invaluable.

Breaking from his thoughts, Harry smiled as he saw Beatrice enter the dormitory and say cheerfully, 'Merry Christmas.'

The next present was a scruffy, slightly battered package from the Queen Mother. Inside was a hand-crafted wooden wind-up rabbit. He turned the key, and the rabbit hopped awkwardly across the bedspread. Harry smiled, touched by the thoughtful, if slightly odd gift.

The third present was from Beatrice's mum, Fergie. It was a large, rattling box that made Beatrice groan the moment she saw it.

'Oh no,' she said, burying her face in her hands.

Harry opened it with curiosity and revealed a bright red Fergie-branded juicer machine.

'Er, thanks?' Harry said, bewildered.

'Sorry,' Beatrice groaned with an embarrassed wince. 'Mum thought she'd strike it big with a line of juicers. It didn't exactly pan out, and now she gives them away to anyone who'll take them.'

Harry laughed and shrugged, 'Well, maybe I'll use it at some point,' though he wasn't quite sure when.

The last present had no label but was neatly wrapped with

a crimson ribbon. As Harry carefully opened it, a luxurious piece of red and white ermine fur flowed out.

Beatrice gasped. 'That's an Infallibility Cloak!' she breathed, her voice hushed with awe. 'If you wear that, you can do *anything*, go *anywhere*, and no one can challenge you. It's like an ultimate shield of authority.'

Harry held it up, the soft fur shimmering in the morning light. There was a small note attached, written in an elegant hand.

> *This cloak was your father's.*
> *Your uncle could make good use of it,*
> *but it is to be passed down to you.*
> *You'll look swell.*

Neither the note nor the packaging had a signature. Harry stared at the handwriting, wondering who it was from.

Beatrice urged him to try the Cloak on, so he draped it over his shoulders. The moment he did, he reached out to take one of Beatrice's chocolates that she had just unwrapped, and though she opened her mouth to object, she seemed to change her mind, simply nodding and looking away.

'It's real,' Harry murmured, astonished.

For the rest of the day, they relaxed in front of the open fire and played with their presents. Later, Harry, Beatrice, Fred, Gabs, and a few other students who had stayed at Balmoral, went down to the Ballroom, which was decked out with crystal baubles and ice sculptures.

Before they could sit down, however, Micheal Fawcett intercepted them.

'Over here,' he drawled, pointing at a large brass weighing scale. 'I hope you are not forgetting our traditions; before you gorge yourself on Christmas supper, you must be weighed. And after, we shall weigh you again.'

Harry, a little unsettled asked, 'Why?'

Curtly, Fawcett replied, 'How else are you to know that you enjoyed your meal?'

Looking at Beatrice with confusion, Harry obliged, writing down his weight as he stood on the weighing platform and then finding a seat. The long dining table groaned under the excess of an incredible spread of food. There were entire roasted geese, enormous cuts of venison dripping with rich gravy, mountains of roast potatoes, Yorkshire puddings as big as a hamper, and decadent dishes of cranberry sauce, bread sauce, and stuffing. For dessert, an army of flaming Christmas puddings was paraded in, carried by footmen dressed as Victorian carollers, and there were towers of mince pies, shortbread biscuits shaped like swans, and even a gigantic gingerbread replica of Balmoral Castle.

The games and traditions, though, were what really made the day extraordinary. After the meal, Prince Philip entertained everyone with his traditional sharp-tongued quips, mostly at the expense of the professors and staff, starting with Sir Robert Fellowes.

'I do apologise, good sir, about all of the extra curating that my *escapades* have caused you with the Royal Archives,' Prince Philip said acerbically. 'I see you've added another drawer to my section of the royal bastards – now, you are sure that these files will stay ... away from prying eyes,' he said snidely, looking around for Piers Morgan.

'Oh yes, of course sir,' Sir Robert said in an unbothered tone. 'On the morose occasion of your death, your will shall be sealed for 90 years. You can leave all money and whatever else to whomever you like, and no plebs will ever know.'

Piers Morgan who was sat not far away and had been pretending not to listen, could not help himself interject.

'I must admit, I have wondered about that,' he said petulantly. 'Not that I would ever *use* the information, but I have been frustrated in previous attempts to get official reasons why certain wills are untouchable. I thought that in

British law, all wills were meant to be publicly available, to prevent corruption, you see.'

Sir Robert Fellowes gave him a disgusted look.

'Exactly,' he said. 'That is why it has been convention for centuries: to protect the dignity of our betters. You are correct about the law, but why would they apply to the royals? I simply request that the courts seal the will and, helpfully, they even block the reasons *why* from being reported. You and your troublesome Fleet Street chums can concern yourself with stories more consummate to your vacuous readers.'

The Queen, who was sat quietly next to Prince Philip stood up abruptly.

'Thank you for that, Sir Robert,' she said tersely, draining her drink. 'As you remind us all, the public need to be satisfied, or they may get restless. Today of all days, they need us – they need me. I hope the young heirs here are paying attention. The public see what they want to see, but they are told what we want them to be told.'

She paused, taking time to look at the students sat interspersed around the table, her gaze ending on Harry.

'Now, I know that the annual Queen's Speech can be a little dry,' she said wryly, picking up Prince Philip's glass and downing it. 'But I cannot understate how important this yearly occasion is to our family's supremacy. An empire can rule by military power or by authoritarian domination – but that is costly, and frankly tiresome. Why do that, when we can achieve the same subservience, funding, admiration and luxury by simply doing one, well-crafted speech a year. It might sound vapid, contrite and condescending to you all here, but the public, *my* public, adore it. My message brings light to their damp council estates, eloquence to their soap opera-infested televisions and, most importantly, meaning to their insignificant lives. Now, if you will excuse me, it is time.'

The Queen strode purposefully away from the table and left the room. For a while, there was a reverential silence as everyone, young and old at the table, reflected on what she had said.

After a while, things got livelier again. The Queen Mother got fully into the spirit of things, donning a paper crown from a Christmas cracker and pretending to knight Fred with her turkey drumstick, declaring him the 'Knight of Rotund Table.' She challenged Beatrice to a game of charades, only to cheat outrageously by mouthing the words of her clues while everyone pretended not to notice.

Harry felt a warmth spread through him that had nothing to do with the roaring fires. This, he thought, was what Christmas was supposed to be about: absurd, ridiculous, over-the-top, but full of laughter and family.

Back in the common room, Harry was waiting for the castle to quieten down and the candles in the hallways to dim. The others had gone to sleep, exhausted by the day's events, but Harry's mind was still lingering on his new cloak. He had left it folded up neatly in his wardrobe, but he couldn't resist the urge any longer. This was his chance to explore the Royal Archives and find the answers he'd been searching for.

He took the Cloak out and draped it over his shoulders, feeling an immediate surge of authority and infallibility. As he stood in front of the mirror, he saw how the ermine fur seemed to ripple with an inner light, and he felt an overwhelming sense of power. As he made his way down the darkened corridors of Balmoral, he couldn't help but strut, his steps growing more confident with each passing moment.

When he reached the door to the Royal Archives, he felt no hesitation as he pushed it open. It swung wide without a creak, as if the very wood recognised his right to be there. The room was vast, lined with tall shelves that reached all the way to the ceiling, each filled with ancient-looking tomes, musty scrolls, and dusty leather-bound volumes. As he stepped inside, the air seemed to whisper with secrets, and Harry couldn't help but feel like he had stepped into the heart of something ancient and forbidden.

He began to browse, taking in the titles of various files and binders, and soon realised quite how much was hidden away from the public eye. There were entire drawers dedicated to notorious and controversial subjects. One cabinet, Harry saw, had his father's name on it.

> *The Black Spider Memos.*
> *Prince Charles' secret lobbying letters to the government.*

Harry rifled through, keen to learn more about his father. His spirits faltered, however, as he saw the headers – one about eradicating all badgers from the United Kingdom, and another about forcing the NHS to fund herbal remedies instead of proper medicine. Seeing that there were twenty-seven in total and concluding that they probably wouldn't contain what he was looking for, Harry moved on, dejected.

Another shelf caught his eye, with the label *Operation Legacy – The End of Empire Files*. Harry remembered from History of Majesty lessons, how all the official documents that detailed the wrongdoings and injustices by the British Empire had to be destroyed, so that ex-colonies could never seek reparations. Harry realised that they hadn't been destroyed – they were all here. The cabinets and drawers went up to the rafters.

Harry wondered aloud, 'If they were hidden away, then then must contain horrible things ... but there are so many ...'

Further down the aisle, he came across folders labelled with names of forgotten royal family members. *The Bowes-Lyon Cousins – Institutional Records* attracted his attention, referring to the Queen Mother's nieces, who had been sent to a mental institution in the 1940s and effectively erased from royal history. Harry shuddered, appreciating with a daunting fear, how even blood relatives had been discarded when they didn't fit the image the family wanted to project.

One particularly large, steel-bound container drew his gaze, simply labelled *The Royal Bastards – Complete Register*. Harry marvelled at how enormous it was. How many could there be, he wondered, dumbfounded.

Moving to the next aisle, Harry came across a huge chest, the lid adorned with the label *Queen's Consent*. Picking up a piece of paper resting on top, he read a note: *One does not consent to these pesky laws*. Below this was a table listing all the laws the Queen had secretly vetoed. Harry gaped, seeing that there were over a thousand listed in the index.

'Well, that answers that question,' he chuckled to himself, as he found the one about the Heat Network Act that he had heard the professors moaning about previously. He also saw, with disquiet, many, many others that related to concealing the Queen's private wealth.

He moved deeper into the archives and came across a record player with an old vinyl LP beside it. The label read: *Prince Philip's Mic-Drop Speech – Kent 1971*.

Without thinking, Harry placed the needle on the record, curious about what the speech might include.

As it began to play, the room was suddenly filled with a blaring rendition of Prince Philip's voice saying, 'And that's why they should all be put on a bloody island and left to sort themselves out!'

The acoustics of the room made the echo deafening and Harry scrambled to lift the needle.

'Blasted thing,' Harry winced. He quickly replaced the record but as he did, he heard voices approaching.

Panic set in, and he clutched the ermine robes around himself. He turned, and through the flickering torch light, he saw Michael Fawcett and Prince Philip striding through the library towards him. They paused, tensing as they caught sight of Harry's shadowed form.

'Who's there?' Fawcett barked.

Harry stood his ground, refusing to let his fear show. He puffed out his chest and furled the Cloak tightly around him, chin lifted with the regal indifference he'd seen so many royals wear as armour. He sauntered out of the Royal Archives section, right past them, deliberately slowing his stride, and gave them a dismissive look, as though they were of no consequence. For a moment, Philip's eyes seemed to bore into him, a flicker of recognition ... but then he blinked, looking confused. Fawcett's face, which had been rigid with annoyance, softened into a blank expression. They both turned away, talking amongst themselves as though Harry had never been there. The Cloak's power, it seemed, was as absolute as Beatrice had said.

Heart pounding, Harry pranced down the corridor, drunk with power, strutting as if he owned the castle. He had almost reached the staircase leading back to the Plantagenet's tower when, in his bluster, he flung open a door at random, a walked blithely inside.

He found himself in a small chamber that he did not recognise. The room was solely lit by a single candelabrum, and at its far end stood a massive, arched frame. Hanging from it was a magnificent tapestry, woven in shimmering threads of gold, crimson, and deep sapphire. Across the top there was stitching that read:

Names written in history, woven in time,
Witness our dynasty, our ascent and our climb.
To assist your journey, behold our deeds and affairs,
To the righteous and worthy, this tapestry shares.
The path to your birthright requires crown, sceptre and stone,
Avoid the scandal and plight of one's desires on the way to the throne.
Do not look too closely at the lives that we led,
It's best to leave our history buried with the dead.
Thank god that society ignores it so blissfully,
As meekly and as silently as the heirs in these threads.

Harry gazed at the tapestry, entranced by its intricate details.

The golden threads that wove through centuries of history gleamed in the faint light, shifting and shimmering as if they were alive, twisting around one another to create the grand family tree of the royal lineage.

The lines stretched upwards, branching out into four distinct directions, each leading to the name of one of the great royal houses: Plantagenet, Tudor, Stuart, and Hanover. The threads flowed like rivers through the centuries and their monarchs, converging at the Queen's name, before fading slightly into the outline of his father's name, Charles. But unlike the others, Charles' threads seemed frayed, tangled, and disrupted, as if his destiny had been rewritten and then left to unravel. Harry could see his own golden line snaking down from Charles's name, running parallel to Will's – the two threads intertwining, circling one another but never merging. It was clear they were bound together, yet also separate, destined to follow different paths.

His heart skipped a beat as he took it all in, the tapestry seeming to whisper the weight of his family's history, of his duty, his destiny. He wondered why this was here. Even compared to the paintings and artefacts that decorated the castle's corridors, this stood out as special. This was older, more important. He felt that by even looking at it, he might reveal secrets that were meant to be concealed. Part of him wanted to turn around and leave, but he was rooted to the spot, transfixed.

He heard a noise echoing from the corridor, jolting him out of his trance and, even with the ermine Cloak, he knew it was time to go. He hurried back to his dormitory, aching for sleep, but his mind could not let go of what he'd seen.

The next morning, he told Beatrice about the tapestry, trying to describe every intricate detail. She listened carefully, frowning at his intensity, and asked if he was all right.

Harry shrugged, forcing a smile. 'It's, I don't know – it felt like I was seeing everything for the first time,' he confessed.

But he brushed it off, pretending that the significance hadn't taken root in him.

Still slightly unsure, Beatrice agreed to go with him later, to see the tapestry for herself.

That evening, Harry led the way back, draping the Cloak around them both as they tiptoed through the corridors. They found the room with ease, and Harry excitedly motioned Beatrice to the tapestry.

'Look,' he said, pointing to the golden threads, 'it's all here.'

Beatrice took in the sight, but her eyes drifted beyond Harry's line, noticing the other threads that sprawled out across the fabric.

'I didn't see this yesterday,' Harry muttered, perplexed. Beatrice, her fingers trembling slightly, traced her own lineage, running her hand up through her father's name, before coming to rest at the Queen's.

'It's beautiful,' she whispered, tracing the bold, elegant lines of Elizabeth I and the commanding presence of Richard the Lionheart. 'All this history, all these people ... it's amazing.'

For a long while, they sat in silence, the enormity of their shared heritage resonating with them. Beatrice pointed to where their threads hung at the bottom of the tapestry.

'You and Will,' she said thoughtfully, 'you're at the centre now. But it's odd, isn't it? You're both on equal footing here. Will should be ... more prominent, but he's not.'

Harry nodded; he had noticed the same thing. After a little while longer, Beatrice touched Harry's elbow and motioned that they should go. They left the room together, but the tapestry stayed with him, burnt into his thoughts.

The next day, Beatrice tried to distract him, suggesting another round of Monopoly, but she could see that his heart wasn't in it. She knew he would go back, even if she didn't.

That night, Harry found himself standing before the tapestry again, unable to resist its call. He settled onto the floor, staring at the golden threads, tracing his finger over them once more, as if by doing so, he could unlock the secrets it held. He barely noticed the shadow that fell across him until a solemn, yet kind voice interrupted his thoughts.

'Back again, Harry?'

He turned sharply and there stood the Queen herself. She was smiling, but there was a melancholy behind her eyes, as they shifted from Harry to the tapestry hanging behind him.

He jumped to his feet, suddenly unsure if he was in trouble or should use the cloak's power to escape.

But before he could act, she laughed softly.

'That cloak won't work on me, my dear,' the Queen said. 'It may gift temporary infallibility, but only I am the sovereign. Only I am truly infallible ... for now.'

Her voice trailed off as her sapphire blue eyes fell from the topmost name down to her own. She stepped closer, and Harry, unsure whether to be embarrassed or defiant, allowed himself to relax a little. Standing beside Harry, as they both looked together towards the names woven into the fabric before them, a gentle, almost wistful expression crossed her face.

'I see you've found the Tapestry of Heirs-in-Thread,' she said, gesturing to the weaving with a slight tilt of her head. 'You've taken in the family's grand history, I expect?'

'It's ... marvellous,' he admitted. 'But why is the end all so tangled? It looks frayed, like something has gone wrong.'

The Queen sighed, studying the threads.

'This tapestry was created many centuries ago ... but continues to unfurl. Your father's name was once where yours now is. But, as his thread shows,' she reached out and rested a white-gloved finger next to her son's name, 'the future is not written, it is not ensured. As you can see from the names of the houses before you, the crown is there to be won and lost. The Windzors rule today, but it has not always been so. Our family follows on from other superior bloodlines; the Saxe-Coburg-Gothas, the Hanovers, the Stuarts. It is easy to view our lineage as a single, unbroken line. But the truth is, every golden thread here represents choices, mistakes, sacrifices, triumphs and losses. As you heard on your first day here, each branch of our history and those that defined it have strengths, but also weaknesses.'

Her hand quivered and briefly hovered over Prince Andrew's name.

'Each of us have choices, those that we do and do not take. They are laid bare before us here, shaping this tapestry and our legacy. The trick is not to let the threads get too tangled or to allow them to become threadbare.'

She paused, her eyes drifting to the lines extending down from Charles.

'Loose threads,' she murmured. 'Those are the most dangerous. They can unravel everything if one is not careful.'

Harry felt a lump in his throat, and before he could stop himself, he asked, 'Is that why I've been brought back?'

The Queen's face softened. 'You are eleven years of age now Harry. And whilst I wanted you to enjoy a quiet childhood, it was always arranged that you would return to us and take your rightful place in our family.'

After a few seconds Harry asked, 'What must I do?'

'Your duty, Harry,' she stated earnestly.

Looking into her eyes, Harry now understood the reverence that the Queen inspired. This small, dainty woman exuded such authority that her presence filled the room, and him, with fealty. But he still needed to know more.

'But if I have a role in all this, then why does Will ... I don't understand why he treats me like ...'

His words faltered as he did not know how to explain their rivalry, or if it was wise to criticise him in front of the Queen. Will was, after all, next in line to the throne, her throne.

Looking intently at Harry, her eyes only a little higher than his, she answered with her quiet, considered voice, 'Although you are just as much a Windzor as Will or I, your childhood has been quite different. Ever since that day when your parents died, you and your brother have started down different paths. Like the Stuarts and Plantagenets of your forbears, they follow different routes, but both end up at the same place.'

The Queen traced her fingertip down the threads connecting her father, King George VI and his older brother, the ill-fated and ill-suited King Edward VIII, through her name, then Prince Charles, and finally coming to rest between Harry and Will's names.

'It is not easy to be the heir, especially when so young. Your brother knows what this means, what he must achieve, and I believe I am correct when I say that he is a little bit ... insecure.'

Her quick, almost mischievous flash of a grin told Harry that she did not mean this unkindly but was instead meant to encourage him. She turned back to him, her face full of something akin to pride.

'You are a part of that future, Harry, as is your brother. Never forget that. We all have our roles to play.'

She placed a gentle hand on his shoulder.

'This tapestry will be moved tomorrow. I suggest you do not seek it out again. But, if your path does lead you back to it,' she added with a knowing smile, 'you will be ready.'

She then turned and walked away, leaving Harry alone with the tapestry, the threads still sparkling in the moonlight.

He stood there for a moment longer, taking in his lineage once more, and as he did, he felt a quiet resolve settle over him. Seeing his name here, following on from such historic people, finally made him accept that he did belong here. He would be somebody, he *was* somebody. But, looking again at his father's name, he knew that he would have to prove himself, stake his claim.

— CHAPTER THIRTEEN —

Laurens van der Post

Harry found himself still haunted by the sight of the tapestry over the remaining days of the Christmas holiday. The name of his father, Prince Charles, tangled in the threads of the woven fabric nagged at him, and he couldn't shake the thought of what sort of king his father might have been. And then there was his mother, Diana, completely absent from it, almost as if she had been erased from history entirely. His conversation with the Queen had initially made him feel more assured of himself and his place at Balmoral. But there were things that she had said, especially about Will, that left him with more questions. However, despite these lingering thoughts, Harry had tucked the Infallibility Cloak away in the depths of his wardrobe, resolving not to use it again anytime soon.

When Zara returned to Balmoral for the new term, Harry and Beatrice recounted everything that had happened over Christmas. Zara listened raptly as they described the tapestry and the search for Laurens van der Post in the Royal Archives.

'Surely you must have found something useful,' she said, visibly frustrated. 'I bet his name is buried in there somewhere!'

'I tried,' Harry said despondently. 'I looked in loads of things, but it would take decades to go through all of those scandals properly.' He scratched his chin irritably and said, 'I know I've seen the name before. It's on the tip of my tongue, but I just can't place it.'

*

At the Plantagenet's next hunting practice, Benjamin announced the unwelcome news that Prince Philip would be overseeing the scoring between them and the Hanovers. Apparently, Philip had been underwhelmed by the overall haul from the previous hunt and was going to set a minimum quota this time. He would be supervising the Gamekeepers before and during the hunt, making them set out more traps and snares than usual and keeping a close watch on the count.

There was a collective groan amongst the group. As the head of the Stuart house, Philip's influence over the scoring felt like a direct challenge, and none of them expected fair treatment.

'But why?' Fred complained. 'He'll only use it as an excuse to undermine us. There's no way we'll stand a chance with him in charge.'

Harry felt the same unease. Not only did he worry that the Plantagenets would be disadvantaged, he also worried about himself. He still had a mark on his hand from when the rifle misfired last time, the one that Philip had handed to him at the start of the previous hunt. The thought of Philip having an even bigger part of the upcoming one unnerved him.

When he returned to the common room that evening, he shared the news with Beatrice and Zara.

'It can't be a coincidence,' Beatrice said firmly. 'Philip wouldn't bother to take the role of the count from Piers Morgan without a personal reason. He's definitely planning something.'

'Maybe you shouldn't take part,' Zara suggested. 'You could come up with some excuse. It's not worth it if he's going to try to trip you up.'

Harry shook his head. 'I can't back out now, how would I explain it to the others? I'll just keep my distance from him.'

Trying to lift his spirits, Zara pulled out a gift she had brought back from her holiday. It was a box of Chocolate

Pogs. She handed them one each. Harry, after unwrapping it, glanced at the disk of chocolate before going to take a bite.

Then he froze, his breath caught in his throat as he recognised the engraving. There, etched into the chocolate, was the face of Prince Charles. It was the same as the first Pog he had ever had. He then turned it over to read the description on the back. As before, it summarised Prince Charles's life, mentioning his death in a car crash with Diana and his controversial interests in pseudoscience and magic. But then, realisation dawned on him as he read on, now aloud to Beatrice and Zara.

'Listen to this: "Prince Charles ... he achieved a 2:2 in History *and collaborated with his mentor, Laurens van der Post on alternative medicine and the legendary powers of historical artefacts.*"!'

Harry looked up and exclaimed, 'That's it! I *knew* I'd seen his name before. I got one of these Pogs on the Balmoral Express. Van der Post – he was one of my dad's mentors!'

Zara stared into the fireplace, thinking.

'The legendary powers of historical artefacts – wait, hold on.'

She reached into her bag, digging through her things before pulling out a heavy book, its title emblazoned on the front in large, gold, curly letters: *From Thrones with Stones to Fools with Jewels: Best Bling for a Wannabe King.*

'I got this for Christmas,' she said happily. 'I bet this has something to do with all this.'

The three huddled around the book as Zara flipped through the pages. She squeaked as she saw Van de Post's name on a page opposite a black and white photo of a large block of stone.

'Look, here he is! Laurens van der Post,' she whispered dramatically, 'has long advocated for the mysterious and miraculous powers *of the Stone of Scone!*'

'The Stone of what?' said Harry and Beatrice together.

'Do neither of you pay attention in History of Majesty?'

They both looked at her sarcastically.

'Look at this,' she said, pointing to a passage that read:

The Stone of Scone has been used during coronations for generations, conferring royal legitimacy. Furthermore, it is believed that the Stone has unlimited healing powers. It has even been rumoured that it can bring people back from the dead.

Harry then saw the photo opposite.

'Wait – that picture of it,' he said. 'That's what was in the vault, I'm sure of it!'

'You saw it? But –' started Beatrice, but Harry cut in.

'Yeah, sort of. It was covered, but it was that exact shape. That's it. That's what the corgis are protecting!'

The three of them were quiet for a few moments, poring over the chapter.

Then Beatrice said slowly, 'So this is what Philip wants? A big, old stone?'

'A stone that apparently has *powers* ...' Zara said, chewing her lip, unsure.

Harry stared down at the photo. It didn't look magical; it didn't look extraordinary at all. It was just a rough, grey oblong, about the size of a suitcase.

'Do you think that's why Philip is after it?' Harry asked quietly. 'Does he want to use it to bring my father back, so that he can be heir again? He must think that neither me nor Will is cut out to be a prince, let alone a king.'

Beatrice put her hand on Harry's.

'No Harry, I'm sure that's not it. I know he's harsh on you he doesn't think that. And anyway, surely bringing your father back isn't possible – and if it was, wouldn't the Queen want that too? Why would Philip be stealing it from her?'

Zara, still reading, suddenly gasped.

'There's more: "Laurens van der Post had much influence over British politicians and royalty. Over time, he became so significant in Prince Charles's life that he even became Prince Will's godfather." Oh.'

'Wait ...' Harry said, stunned. 'If he's this connected to the royal family, why haven't we found anything about him in the library?'

'Because,' Zara continued, her lips thinning, 'it says here he was involved in a scandal. In 1953, during a sea voyage to England he was meant to be the guardian of a fourteen-year-old girl. But ... he abused, impregnated and then abandoned her ... that's probably why there's no mention of him anywhere. When this story finally came out, they must have erased him from the records.'

Beatrice shivered, shaking her head. 'Our fathers have odd choices in friends, don't they?'

Harry's thoughts churned.

'I still don't understand why Philip wants this Stone. Healing powers, bringing people back from the dead, and used in coronations? I mean, it sounds like either he wants to bring back my dad, or somehow, an old historic monarch to rule again.'

Beatrice couldn't help but let out a wry laugh and say, 'Well, us Windzors aren't exactly as popular as the papers make out, are we? Maybe getting Elizabeth I back for a bit wouldn't hurt.'

'Or,' said Zara conspiratorially, 'there is another possibility. If the Stone is as powerful as the book suggests, then maybe it can grant immortality along with divine right – maybe Philip wants the throne for himself ... and to rule, for ever!'

Harry and Beatrice both laughed but then stopped quickly, seeing that Zara wasn't joining in.

'You know there have been rumours,' Zara continued quietly, her eyes sweeping the common room. 'Apparently Philip hasn't always been happy playing second fiddle to the Queen. A man like him, maybe he wants more than to be merely Prince Consort.'

After an uncomfortable silence, Harry said, 'Whatever

powers that Stone may have, we can't let him get it. I'm just glad those corgis are protecting it.'

*

In the days leading up to the next hunt, the tension between Harry and Prince Philip only grew more palpable. Prince Philip took every opportunity to belittle and undermine Harry during their Mixology lessons, critiquing even the smallest mistake with a venomous tone.

'Careful, boy, add any more ginger to that and we'll have to call it The Fergie,' Philip sneered one day as Harry carefully grated the root.

He kept his head down but wondered: did Philip somehow know they suspected him? Or was he spitefully trying to keep Harry on edge before the upcoming competition?

To add to Harry's worries, at the end of the lesson, Prince Philip brought up the topic of exams. The class moaned as Philip set them the homework of memorising which fruit slices best adorned different cocktails. Harry followed the others out of the cellar, now in a particularly bad mood.

*

Finally, the day of the hunt arrived. Harry could feel the anticipation crackling in the air as the students and staff gathered near the hunting lodge, their breath visible in the chilly morning.

Harry felt a huge relief when he saw the Queen herself had come to watch the proceedings; maybe with her there, Philip wouldn't be able to pull any tricks. Still, Harry knew he needed to finish this hunt as quickly as possible before anything could go wrong.

Prince Philip, standing on a raised platform, cleared his throat and announced the prize kill for the day's hunt.

'Today, our Plantagenet and Hanover Stalkers will be aiming for a hen harrier.'

A ripple of appreciation ran through the crowd.

Someone joked, 'Good luck Stalkers, that'll save me using

up my poison.'

Harry tried to ignore the raucous laughter and instead steel himself for what he had to do. Would it be easier than last time he wondered – the image of the collapsing stag flashing through his mind.

The competition began, and Harry tried to block out the distractions around him, focusing on the task at hand, resolute in what he had to do. Meanwhile, Zara and Peter Phillips were enduring Will's taunts, his voice carrying over the murmurs of the crowd.

'You Phillips' are not even proper royals,' he said, smirking. 'Your mum gave up your titles. You're just commoners playing dress-up.'

Zara reacted angrily, but Beatrice stepped in. 'Get lost, Will. There's more to life than titles. Or maybe that's why you are so insecure; what would you be if you weren't the heir?'

Determined not to let the distractions get to him, Harry moved quickly away from the lodge and hurried to the top of a bare hill with a clear view of the sky. He scanned the surroundings, watching the Gunners taking aim at the quail fluttering around as he paused to inspect his gun, checking for any signs of tampering. He had an uneasy feeling that he was being closely watched.

Harry moved on, eyes straining against the cold sky and ears alive to any distant bird cry. Hearing applause in the distance he wondered which party was winning. Would Philip be counting the birds fairly? At least, he reasoned, if he got the prize kill quickly, it would end the hunt, and some quail would be spared. He emerged through a copse and raised his head, the frigid air tingling his nose.

And then, there it was! A male hen harrier, soaring gracefully against the blue sky. Without pausing to think, Harry took his shot. There was a sharp crack, and then the bird fell from the sky.

He'd done it.

A quiet fell on the estate as the onlookers in the distance realised what had happened, their attention grabbed by the distinctive gunshot. Then, as Harry watched the lifeless bird crumple into the hard ground, he heard people erupt into applause, rushing towards him and congratulating him on his incredible aim. Plantagenets swarmed round, celebrating and singing. But as the excitement slowly died down, Harry felt the familiar guilt. Hen harriers were incredibly rare and seeing its beautiful feathers, broken and splayed, left him feeling empty.

The competition officially ended with the Plantagenets declared winners, but the bloodlust of the crowd hadn't been sated. People lingered, continuing to shoot at the other game birds roaming the area.

Unsettled, Harry handed in his gun and made his way to the nearby woods, needing a moment of solitude. He found a quiet spot beneath a large oak and sat down, resting his head against the rough bark. The image of the bird falling was ingrained in his eyes.

Voices drifted through the trees, snapping him out of his thoughts. He stiffened and, peering through the foliage, he saw Prince Philip and Piers Morgan standing in a secluded clearing. Harry kept as still as he could, straining to hear their conversation.

'Don't play games with me, Morgan,' Philip was saying, his voice threatening. 'The Stone of Scone is too important to be the subject of frivolous tales. You know something, something you've learnt from all those answer phone messages.'

Piers Morgan shifted uncomfortably, looking as though he'd rather be anywhere else.

'I don't know what you're talking about,' he said.

'Oh, don't be coy,' Philip said scornfully. 'Your paper has been tapping phones for years. You know things that only a select few should be aware of. Things that, if let slip, could have dire consequences. And you know I'm talking about more than just another royal affair.'

Morgan's face paled, but he managed to maintain his composure. 'I've already told you, I don't know anything about this Stone, and I have no idea why anyone would care about it anyway. I'm a journalist, not a geologist.'

Philip stepped closer, his voice dropping to a menacing growl. 'If you think I won't find out who you've been leaking to this time, you're mistaken. I'll be waiting for you to change your mind and come clean.'

With a snarl of his lip, Philip turned on his heel and strode away, leaving Piers Morgan looking more rattled than ever.

Harry stayed hidden until Morgan regained his composure and disappeared in the opposite direction. Once he was sure the coast was clear, Harry made his way back to the castle and up to the common room, where Zara and Beatrice were waiting, wondering where he had got to.

After shaking off other students praising him on his fine shot during the hunt, he found a quiet corner to conspire with the others. Breathlessly, he recounted everything he had seen and heard.

'So, it definitely *is* the Stone that is being guarded by the three corgis?' Zara said, frowning. 'And Prince Philip thinks Piers Morgan knows something about it?'

'It must be more than that though,' Beatrice added thoughtfully. 'If Philip is worried about more people knowing about it, and maybe even knowing about its powers, then maybe others might be after it too!'

'No wonder Philip's temper is getting worse then,' Harry said mockingly. 'Every day that goes by that he doesn't get his hands on the Stone, the more likely he'll be beaten to it.'

'Especially with Piers Morgan in the know,' added Beatrice.

Zara nodded solemnly.

They fell silent, each pondering what Morgan and Prince Phillip's plans were. Oblivious to the upbeat clamour around them, as their fellow Plantagenets continued to revel in their hunt victory, they sat staring at the fire, restless and troubled.

— CHAPTER FOURTEEN —

Karen the Komodo Dragon

The Easter holidays passed in a blur of textbooks, essays and late-night study sessions as Harry, Zara, and Beatrice huddled in the library. The impending exams dominated their thoughts, but they still made time to keep a discreet eye on Piers Morgan.

His usual rosy-cheeked appearance had become paler and more drawn, but they assumed that he was holding out, despite whatever pressure Philip might have been putting on him.

Exam revision, however, was relentless. They spent hours cramming for their Deference Towards the Monarchs class. They had to memorise instances of media scandals that had not been kept under wraps and make notes on what false stories could have been written to distract from them more successfully.

Beatrice went red when they got to the example of the story about Fergie being photographed having her toes sucked by her financial advisor last year, during her protracted separation from Prince Andrew.

Po-faced, Harry said, 'I'm not sure what to suggest for this story as a distraction piece, maybe Elvis coming back from the dead?'

Zara giggled, 'Maybe that's what Philip wants the Stone of Scone for.'

Still blushing, Beatrice shot back at Harry, 'I assume you've forgotten about that infamous phone recording between your dad and *her* then?'

Harry's grin faltered. 'What recording, what do you mean?'

For a second Beatrice looked triumphant, but Harry's vulnerable expression tempered her.

'Well, you surely know about your dad's, er, history with *her*?' Beatrice said and Harry nodded. 'Well, one of their more intimate phone calls was recorded, and the press released it ... Prince Charles, he said some weird things, something about wanting to die and be reincarnated as something living in her trousers.'

'Oh,' said Harry bleakly. 'That does explain a couple of things though. My Uncle Charles really does hate the press, and if it was stuff like that, then I don't blame him. It must have been horrible for my mum.'

Zara and Beatrice smiled sadly at Harry. He didn't often mention his mum, but they both knew that her absence still really affected him.

'It also explains why Piers Morgan always has that annoying air when around me, like he knows secrets about me or something. I bet he loved that story,' Harry said bitterly.

They moved on to their Smarms homework. They had to commit to memory phrases that commoners might say to them during engagements, ensuring that they knew what they meant, to not hinder any small talk.

Zara was getting more and more frustrated at this until finally, she huffed, 'What exactly is a nine to five?'

Laughing in surprise, Harry answered, 'You know, it's what the servants do. They have shifts from 9am to 5pm.'

With a look of horror, Zara said, 'What! As in they work *all day*?'

Harry nodded sympathetically but quickly refocused. He also had his hands full with Apothecary revision. They all did. Learning recipes for ailments common in the royal family, like gout, was proving tedious. There were just so many diseases.

One afternoon, as they pored over their revision notes, they noticed something odd. The Queen Mother was sheepishly shuffling into the library. It wasn't unheard of, but it was strange enough for them to glance at each other with raised eyebrows.

'What's she doing in here?' Beatrice whispered.

Harry leaned forwards slightly, trying to see which section she was going to. 'Dunno, but we could ask.'

They approached her casually, and as they neared, she spotted them.

'Hello dears, after something are we?' she asked, with a knowing look of mischief.

'Hello Granny,' Harry began, then added, 'we're not still looking for info on Laurens van der Post, if that's what you mean.'

At the mention of Van der Post, the Queen Mother immediately bridled. 'You're not, are you?'

Beatrice chimed in. 'Actually, we already know everything. The scandals, the pseudoscience – and we figured out the biggest piece of the puzzle. It's the Stone of Scone, isn't it?'

The Queen Mother flinched and quickly shushed them, glancing around the room to ensure no one had overheard.

'Hush now! You mustn't go shouting that about,' she said urgently. 'Come see me this evening at my cottage, but I make no promises. We can't have loose lips around here. Make sure you aren't seen leaving the castle.'

As she shuffled away, Harry caught sight of the book she had nonchalantly taken from one of the shelves, *Royal Reptiles: The Fine Art of Rearing Cold-Blooded Companions*.

'That can't be normal,' Harry muttered, shaking his head.

Just then, he noticed Will lurking nearby.

Will had been lingering just long enough to possibly overhear their conversation, and, Harry noticed, Will was also eyeing the book in the Queen Mother's hand as she left. He slunk off with a self-satisfied smirk, leaving Harry with an ominous feeling.

'Will was loitering over there. I'm pretty sure that he heard something,' Harry said in a low voice.

Zara sighed. 'Great, just what we need.'

After dinner, as the sun was setting, they made their way to the Queen Mother's Garden Cottage, eager to hear what she might divulge.

'Come in, dears,' the Queen Mother said, greeting them warmly, though her eyes were guarded.

The cottage had the smell of freshly baked scones alongside something far less pleasant – an acrid, earthy scent of something unusual. They didn't waste time with pleasantries.

'So, what else is guarding the Stone besides your corgis?' Beatrice asked, trying to sound laidback but failing to hide her curiosity.

The Queen Mother's expression was inscrutable.

'Already guessed that there's more than my three little angels then? I honestly have no idea how you even know about them, and I'm not entirely sure that I want to know.'

All three looked awkwardly at the ground, hoping that she didn't press them on this.

'Before I tell you anything else,' she said carefully. 'What *are* you three up to? Now I certainly understand how tough it is to be a young royal whilst keeping away from scandals ... but exams are fast approaching. I don't want you distracted from perfecting your protocol; duties don't do themselves you know.' She said this whilst unable to keep a cheeky grin from twitching the corners of her mouth.

'Granny we are revising hard, look!' Zara said, rummaging in her bag and pulling out a cocktail shaker. 'We've prepared a martini for you, just the way you like it, for your usual evening tipple.'

As Zara poured it for her into a waiting glass, Harry pressed on.

'The thing is, we're distracted because we're worried about the Stone and that someone is after it. We know that you know *everything* that goes on around here, and so we were hoping that you'd put our minds at ease.'

'You do flatter me, don't you?' she smiled, then took a refined sip of her drink, as if deciding whether to indulge them. After a moment, she relented.

'Well, aside from my corgis, of course, there are defences by the Queen herself. And also ... Mark Bolland, Princess Margaret, Princess Anne ... and, yes, Prince Philip.'

They blinked in surprise.

'Philip?' Harry repeated. 'But we thought he might be –'

'Trying to steal it?' the Queen Mother cut in, testily. 'Don't be foolish. Prince Philip is not trying to steal the Stone. Quite the contrary. He's one of the few who understand the dangers.'

'Well, that's a relief,' Zara said, though she didn't seem entirely convinced. 'But can you at least reassure us that no one knows how to get past the corgis, right?'

The Queen Mother raised an eyebrow. 'Only myself and the Queen know that. The corgis are trained in a way you could scarcely imagine.'

As they spoke, Harry's attention was drawn to something large by the fire. With a pang, he realised what he was looking at – it was an egg, an enormous one, resting on a bed of coals. The shell was leathery and had a faint pattern to it.

'Is that ...' Harry began, pointing at the egg, 'a lizard's egg?'

'Or a snake?' asked Zara.

The Queen Mother beamed proudly.

'That, my dears, is a Komodo dragon egg.'

Beatrice's mouth opened in surprise, 'But aren't they endangered? Surely that's not allowed, even for us royals?'

The Queen Mother chuckled, clearly unconcerned with any legalities. 'Oh, come now. Royals have always kept exotic pets. Did you know Edward VII had a pet cheetah? And Princess Michael of Kent had a lynx.' She sniffed contemptuously. 'No one will know anyway; I just wanted a little friend to look after while my three darlings were on guard duty.'

'Aren't they pretty dangerous?' Harry asked.

'Don't worry, I've been doing my homework,' the Queen Mother said, nodding at the Royal Reptiles book Harry had seen her with at the library. 'Komodo dragons can be a bit snappy, but no worse than Princess Margaret before breakfast.'

'Where did you get it from?' Zara asked inquisitively.

'I won it in a drinking competition down at the local pub. Someone challenged me to a few rounds, poor fool – didn't stand a chance. I couldn't believe my luck when he gave me this as the forfeit.'

Just as they were about to enquire further, a loud crack sounded from the egg.

They all turned towards the fire in unison, staring, absorbed. The leathery shell began to split, and small fragments of the egg toppled into the coals. From within, a wriggling, scaly creature began to emerge.

The Queen Mother clapped her hands expectantly, her wrinkled face lighting up with delight.

'There it is!' she exclaimed joyfully. 'Come on, you little beauty!'

A tiny head, followed by a long, muscular body, then a whipping tail pushed through the shell. The baby Komodo dragon blinked at the sudden exposure to the room's warm light, flicking its tongue curiously at the air.

Harry, Zara, and Beatrice gawped, mesmerised by the sight of the newborn reptile. It was surprisingly cute for something destined to grow into one of the world's most dangerous predators.

'What are you going to call it?' Beatrice asked.

'Karen,' the Queen Mother said firmly. 'A strong name for a strong female character,' as she leaned over to stroke her head. The creature squirmed a bit under her touch, then relaxed, nuzzling into the warmth of her palm.

'Surely, though,' Beatrice continued cautiously, 'you can't actually keep a Komodo dragon, even here. I mean, they're dangerous. And rare. What if someone does find out?'

The Queen Mother's delighted expression waned for the briefest moment, before smiling again as the baby put its delicate webbed front foot on her finger.

Transfixed on Karen, her forked tongue darting in and out and the orange of the log fire dancing off her small, glistening eyes, the four of them sat quietly, watching. Only the crackle of the fire and small squeaks from the baby dragon broke the cosy atmosphere of the cottage.

Harry then felt the hackles on his neck rise, there was another noise. Quickly, he turned round on his seat and there, in the frame of the window, was Will. Will's eyes met Harry's, accompanied with a malevolent grin, then he disappeared.

'Oh,' said the Queen Mother who had also looked up, 'that's not good.' She shook her head before looking sadly back at Karen.

'Will, I do love him, but he'll sell any story to the press. I don't want any headlines about "Royal Reptile Scandal" on the front page of *The Daily Mail*. We all know where those sorts of stories lead ...'

Harry, Beatrice and Zara looked at each other worriedly.

'Anyway,' the Queen Mother said more urgently, 'you three better get back up to the castle, look how late it is. You'd better be in bed before Will goes and finds Piers Morgan.'

They bade the Queen Mother a hasty goodbye and headed back to the castle, moving quickly under the clear night's sky. After sneaking back through the entrance doors, they moved stealthily through the corridors, towards the Plantagenet tower.

As they rounded a corner, they stumbled upon a scene they had not expected. Princess Anne was stood in front of Will, her arms crossed, clearly unimpressed as she reprimanded him.

'Detention, Will,' she said sternly. 'What do you think you were you doing sneaking around at this hour?'

Will, looking flustered and defensive, said, 'I was trying to find you to tell you about Harry! He has a Komodo dragon!'

Princess Anne's eyebrows arched precariously, clearly not buying any of it. 'What nonsense,' she said, grabbing him by the ear and leading him away.

The three of them waited a couple of minutes, until the footsteps had fully receded.

'Come on,' breathed Harry. 'The coast is clear, let's go.'

But, as he took a step, a strong hand clinched him on his shoulder and whipped him round. Harry saw the gleeful face of Michael Fawcet leering above him, a venomous glint in his eyes.

'Well, well, well ... one is in trouble ...'

— CHAPTER FIFTEEN —

The Ballochbuie Forest

Fawcett led Harry, Beatrice and Zara through the castle, his smugness practically radiating with each step. They were headed straight for Princess Anne's study. Harry tried in vain to compose himself, attempting to come up with some explanation, some innocent reason for being found out of bed at this hour. How could they explain this without dragging the Queen Mother and the Komodo dragon into it? He shot a look at the others, whose faces were just as pale and grim. They were trapped.

When they finally arrived, the door opened to reveal Princess Anne seated behind her imposing desk; she looked up with surprise.

Fawcett announced with glee, 'I caught these three sneaking around the castle, Your Highness.'

Anne's mouth pursed in disapproval, and she looked slowly at each of them in turn, her hands now clasped tightly on the desk. Harry half expected her to shout, but her voice was clipped and controlled as she uttered, 'Explain yourselves, now.'

Harry had no answer. He knew that they could not say anything without causing more trouble. He cast a sideways look at Beatrice and Zara, whose downcast eyes were fixed on their own feet, unable to meet the scrutiny of Anne's gaze. As the silence began to feel unbearable, Harry steeled his resolve and decided the throw caution to the wind.

'But I thought the Windzor rule was "Never complain, never explain".'

Princess Anne bridled at once, her neck pulsing and her hands tightening into claws.

'How dare you use our own tactics against me!' she seethed, in a voice so incensed that Harry took a step back. 'Even you must know that only works on the plebs.'

Standing up and towering over Harry, regaining her usual, air of cool authority, she said, 'It's obvious what's happened here. You've concocted some ridiculous plot to frame Will, haven't you? Made up a completely mad story about a Komodo dragon!'

She turned her ire onto the other two.

'I don't know what you all were thinking, but I'll tell you what's going to happen now,' she continued, baring down on them. 'All three of you are getting detention, and you've cost your house fifty points – each! Don't even think about arguing.'

One hundred and fifty points! Harry felt sick to his stomach. He glanced at the others again, who were as horrified as him. There would be no recovering from this. The entire house would turn against them by morning.

Princess Anne sent them away, her lips pressed into a thin line of disappointment. Fawcett led them back to their common room in silence, a vindictive look of delight contorting his spiteful face.

The next morning, the mood in the castle was as bad as they'd expected. Word had spread, and Harry could feel the hostile glares burning into him from every direction. No one knew exactly what had happened, but all that mattered was that three stupid first-years had been caught exploring the castle at night and the Plantagenet house had lost one hundred and fifty points.

Harry had long become accustomed to mixed attitudes from the other students. Now, however, everyone treated him, and Beatrice and Zara, with derision. The Plantagenets, so desperate to finally beat the Stuarts to the House Cup this year, were disgusted with them. Even the Hanovers and Tudors, who had also hoped to see the Stuarts supremacy toppled, treated their group with utter contempt.

The Stuarts were insufferable, muttering things such as, 'Like Fergie like daughter, eh, Beatrice?' and 'No wonder you don't have any titles, Zara.' But Harry faced the brunt of the insults, feeling as low and unwelcome as he had ever been in his life.

They threw themselves into studying for their exams, keeping their heads down as much as possible. It was a relief to focus on something other than the scandal swirling around them. One bit of news, that at least gave them one less thing to worry about, was that the Queen Mother had found someone to take Karen the Komodo dragon.

After they had a quick breakfast one morning, trying to ignore the muttering that followed them, they bumped into the Queen Mother in the entrance hall.

'I've sent Karen to live at Woburn Abbey – the Duke of Bedford said he'd take good care of her,' she told them. 'He's actually quite excited. You see, he's always felt a bit guilty that it was his ancestor, the 11th Duke of Beford, Herbrand Russell, who introduced the grey squirrels to the UK. He gifted so many of the critters to other estates around the country, that he's basically the reason that they are now everywhere and have killed off the beautiful red squirrels. But young Andy Russell, the scoundrel, has a plan. He's going to breed an army of Komodo dragons from Karen and then release them, to eat up all the greys. What could possibly go wrong!'

Harry looked dubiously at the other two.

The Queen Mother left them, heading back to her cottage. And although she had said it was for the best, Harry could see that she'd lost her spring in her step. He also wondered if her tipple timetable had gotten busier; he could hear her hiccupping all the way down the path.

'At least she didn't get into trouble,' Harry said to the other two. 'Will must have realised that he was in enough trouble as well, and so he's dropped it.' Harry was beginning to understand how easy it was to fall into scandal; how a single misstep, a moment of carelessness, could spiral into disaster.

*

One late afternoon, as Harry was walking back from the library alone, he heard something strange coming from a nearby classroom. It was Piers Morgan's voice. Harry stopped in his tracks, listening; Morgan was pleading with someone.

'Please,' Morgan's voice wavered, sounding more desperate than Harry had ever heard. 'I can't – I don't want to do this anymore. It's too dangerous!'

There was a pause, followed by another voice, quiet and so distorted by an electronic buzz, that Harry couldn't make out the words. But it sounded angry.

'Alright, alright, I will,' Morgan finally relented, his voice full of resignation. Harry pressed himself against the wall as Morgan left the classroom, his head down, chuntering to himself as he walked right past Harry, too preoccupied to notice him.

Harry waited for a moment, then peeked into the classroom.

It was empty.

But the door on the other side was slightly open. Whoever Morgan had been talking to must have left that way. Harry was sure it had been Philip, threatening him again.

Later, when he found Beatrice and Zara, he related what had happened.

'I think Morgan's caved,' he said grimly. 'I think Philip has finally broken him.'

Beatrice frowned. 'Should we go to the Queen?'

'No,' Zara said firmly. 'There'd be too much to explain. And do you really think she'd believe us over her husband on something like this?'

*

One dreary evening a few days later, Harry, Zara and Beatrice headed down to the entrance hall to meet Michael Fawcett to start their detention. Next to Fawcett stood Will, looking indignant. Harry, in his own self-pity had forgotten that Will had also received detention. Fawcett, as usual, was smirking with smug satisfaction, clearly enjoying their collective misery.

He led them out into the grounds, his pompous strut irritating Harry with each step. As they walked towards the Garden Cottage, Fawcett couldn't resist gloating.

'You know,' Fawcett began, his tone gleeful, 'I've gotten into my fair share of trouble too. But, of course, never saw much punishment. You have much to learn, little heirs.'

He shot a knowing look at them, relishing the moment as he continued. 'Why, back when I worked with the Prince's Trust, I helped secure some ... let's say, *creative donations*. Nothing too improper, mind you, simply a few mutually beneficial exchanges. Connections can work wonders. Like the time I helped broker that deal for the Qatari investors ... kept things out of the press, naturally.'

Harry exchanged a look with Zara, both of them wondering how someone so unpleasant had managed to avoid any consequences for so long. But Harry knew that this was the way things worked in these circles. You could get away with nearly anything if you had the right friends, and leverage.

As they approached the Queen Mother's cottage, Harry's spirits lifted ever so slightly. Surely, she wouldn't let the punishment be too bad. But noticing Harry's hopefully expression, Fawcett's spoke again, more malicious than ever.

'Oh no,' he said, his smile widening. 'You're not staying at the Queen Mother's cottage tonight. She has a task for you. No ... you're off to the forest.'

Even Will, usually full of arrogant swagger, looked unnerved at that. Harry felt a knot form in his stomach. The

THE BALLOCHBUIE FOREST

Ballochbuie forest was notorious, filled with ancient trees and wild animals. There were reasons that all students were forbidden from going in there.

The Queen Mother, now standing by the gate, gave them a brief, formal greeting.

'Something's been disturbing the royal beehives,' she explained, looking unusually anxious. 'We need to check on them tonight, see what's been going on. You four are coming with me. I must admit though, it may be a bit dangerous – I won't lie.'

She drew her coat around her, inadvertently revealing an old service pistol in a holster on her belt.

Zara, noticing it, asked, 'Where did you get that old thing, Granny?'

'Oh this,' she said, pulling out the gun. 'I've had it since the Second World War. At the time, there was a fear that the Nazis would try to kidnap us, like they did with the King of Belgium. And so,' she said aloofly, 'I was trained in combat and self-defence.'

She twirled the gun round her finger dextrously and slotted it back into her holster. 'If they had managed to reach our shores, I would have given them what for, you best believe it.'

Harry and the others gazed admiringly at her, but Fawcett muttered under his breath, so that the Queen Mother couldn't hear him, 'Maybe you should have had a word with Edward VIII then,' before shuffling off back to the castle.

The four of them followed the Queen Mother into the dense forest, the underbrush crunching beneath their feet as the trees closed in around them. A few minutes in, she stopped suddenly and pointed to a patch of leaves on the ground, glistening with golden liquid in the moonlight.

'See that? That's royal jelly,' she said, sounding upset and a little unnerved. 'This is the food the bees make to feed their queen. It should never be outside the hive. Something, or someone, has been stealing it.'

She motioned for them to move on.

'And it's not only that. I've found dead queen bees, too. Whatever's doing this, is killing them.'

Harry looked around at the gnarled trees surrounding them, straining to see past them into the gloom. The forest suddenly felt even more threatening than it had minutes before.

'We'll split up,' the Queen Mother said after a few more minutes, stopping to consider the forked path before them and turning to face the group.

'Harry, Zara and I will go to one apiary. Will and Beatrice, you check the other.'

Harry nodded obediently, glad to be going with the Queen Mother but giving a Beatrice an apologetic grimace as she followed Will down the other path. They ventured further into the forest, following the narrow, twisting trail that led deeper into the shadows. Along the way, they found more traces of the royal jelly, shining like molten gold against the dark foliage.

'What do you think is doing this?' Harry asked, trying to keep his voice steady. 'There aren't bears left in Scotland, are there?'

The Queen Mother chuckled. 'Bears? No, the Romans got rid of them here by the fifth century. A shame, really. Would've been fun to hunt them, don't you think?'

Zara looked at her quizzically. 'What about wolves?'

'Nope,' the Queen Mother, said with a certain pride in her voice. 'We can take the credit for getting rid of *them*. Back in the thirteenth-century, Edward I ordered their extermination – even appointed a knight to carry out the task. We completely got rid of them in England by Henry VII's reign. Took us till the eighteenth-century to kill off the last ones in Scotland though ... but nothing much survives for long when we are in charge.'

Harry felt the familiar gnawing of shame, suddenly thinking about the hunting competitions he'd taken part in. But the Queen Mother's voice pulled him out of his thoughts.

'Whatever it is,' she said darkly, 'it's worse than bears or wolves.'

Suddenly, breaking the dormant quiet of the forest, the sound of hooves rumbled through the trees, followed by a man's voice.

'Wolves?' the voice called out with a hint of mockery. 'Not around here, I can assure you.'

Out of the gloom emerged a man on horseback, dressed in the garb of the Countryside Alliance. His appearance was pompous and overly grandiose, his nose turned up in an air of superiority. The Queen Mother recognised him immediately.

'Ah, Captain Farquhar,' she greeted pleasantly. 'He leads patrols in these parts for us,' she explained to the children.

The man tipped his hat and launched into a self-important speech. 'We keep these woods clear of any vermin, Your Highnesses. No pine martens, no wildcats. If it doesn't serve a purpose or if it threatens our game, we remove it. Lay snares, traps – take them out before they become a problem. Nature needs a firm hand!'

He droned on, boasting about the various wildlife 'control' measures he'd overseen, his disregard for the forest's ecosystem clear in every word.

The Queen Mother, bored by his familiar monologue, steered the conversation back to the matter at hand.

'Seen anything odd recently?' she asked.

'Nothing out of place ma'am, apart from the disturbed beehives. I shall report to you at once if I find the culprit.'

With a pompous wave, he trotted off, leaving them to continue on their path. The Queen Mother shook her head in exasperation and shrugged her shoulders at the others.

They pressed on, the forest growing darker, more ominous with each step. Harry could feel the damp, undisturbed air seeping through his coat; the gathering mist blanketing everything, deadening the sound of their movements.

Suddenly, a scream echoed through the trees, distant but

unmistakable. The Queen Mother tensed, then bolted towards the sound, her pistol drawn.

Harry and Zara were left standing there, frozen in place, until a few minutes later the Queen Mother reappeared, dragging a bashful Beatrice and an annoyed Will behind her.

'Will decided to scare Bea,' the Queen Mother said crossly. 'Enough folly. Harry, you go with this fool of a prince. Beatrice, you come with us.'

Harry's felt on edge as he and Will walked side by side, deeper into the woods. Will was the last person that he would want with him in this situation, but still, he was glad that he was not alone. After what felt like an eternity, they arrived at a secluded apiary. One of the hives had been knocked over, honey spilling out onto the ground in a sticky mess. There were no bees though – the lack of buzzing made the scene even more disturbing and unnatural.

But there was something else there that was out of place. A figure was moving towards the fallen hive, cloaked and hunched over like some kind of wild animal. It was picking up a bee frame and chewing the wax.

Harry's scar twinged, sending a sudden, searing pain, behind his eyes. He staggered back, clutching his forehead.

The figure stopped mid-motion and looked up, its recessed eyes locking onto his. Harry's breath caught in his throat. The figure's face was shrouded in a hood but in the gloom, Harry caught the glint of two, hateful eyes and the haggard outline of a worn face beneath long, wavy, white hair.

Will screamed and scampered away, leaving Harry standing, immobile, as the cloaked figure began to move towards him, its eyes fixed on him like a predator.

As cold fear flooded through him, a thundering rush of hooves echoed through the trees, and one of the Countryside Alliance horsemen appeared from behind him, leaping over Harry and charging at the figure. The rider's sudden appearance startled the cloaked shape, sending it scurrying back into the depths of the forest.

Harry collapsed to the ground, his head spinning.

The horseman, younger than the previous one, slowed his mount to a stop, and turned to look at Harry. His face was pale, but his voice remained steady as he asked, 'Are you alright?'

Harry nodded, though his head was still pounding from the encounter.

The horseman, catching sight of the crown-shaped scar on Harry's forehead, suddenly seemed to recognise him.

'You're the Windzor boy,' he said poignantly.

Then, glancing nervously around the dark forest, he added, 'We should get you back to the Queen Mother, quickly. You're not safe here.'

Without waiting for a response, the horseman reached down and hoisted Harry onto the horse in front of him. The beast snorted and shuffled restlessly, and they began to move swiftly through the trees. As they picked up speed, the first horseman came galloping out of the darkness, his face twisted in indignation.

'You're letting him share your mount?' he barked. 'Bet the boy doesn't even pay his membership dues to the Countryside Alliance yet. Doesn't deserve the ride.'

The younger horseman shot him a distasteful look.

'I had no choice. He was attacked ...'

The older man's reprimand died in his throat as he registered what had been said. They looked at each other – a worried understanding passing between them. Captain Farquhar's hand whitened as he gripped his reins but said nothing further as the younger horseman spurred his mount forwards, leaving him behind.

They rode in silence for a while, the branches scratching at Harry's face as they weaved through the dense trees. Eventually, the horseman slowed again, pulling the horse to a gentle halt.

Harry, finally getting his breath back, looked round at the man. 'What ... who was that figure?' he asked, his voice trembling.

The horseman looked down at Harry with a strange intensity and did not answer straight away.

'Do you know,' the horseman asked softly, 'what royal jelly is used for?'

Harry nodded his head hesitantly, bewildered by question.

'It's food for the queen bee, isn't it?'

The horseman's gaze sharpened. 'More than that,' he said. 'It's special. If a worker bee is fed nothing but royal jelly, it will become a queen. It will transform, becoming superior to its sisters ... but some people seek this too ...'

Harry stared up at the young but troubled face of the man, lit only by the moonlight.

'But there's an extortionate price to it,' he continued. 'Especially at Highgrove. You must understand, to survive only on this honey ... it warps you. Your teeth will yellow. Your hair will turn white and wild. Your appearance becomes haughty, unnatural. You might gain the title of queen, but you'll never be revered. Never be truly accepted by the people. You'll always be seen as ... underserving.'

'But why would anyone want that?' Harry asked. 'Why would anyone be so desperate?'

'What if this was only a temporary solution?' the horseman answered, quicker now, more urgently. 'What if someone – what if the figure you just saw, only needed this royal jelly for now? What if they were using it to endure, but only until they could find something more powerful, something that could make them a true monarch? A legitimate, accepted ruler?'

'I don't know what you mean – what can do that?' Harry asked. And then it hit him. 'Wait, you don't mean the ... the Stone of Scone?'

The horseman smiled grimly.

'Exactly. The Stone of Scone, or Stone of Destiny as it is

also known, is hidden here at Balmoral. Used in coronations to confer legitimacy, yes. But also rumoured to have certain ... *other properties* ...'

'How do you know about the Stone?' Harry asked, wondering for a panicked second if this horseman was working for Philip.

'The Queen Mother has informed a few of us about it; it is why we are conducting more patrols currently. We are keeping the Balmoral estate safe from more than pesky, unwanted fauna.'

Harry's heart thudded in his chest. It all started to make a sick kind of sense.

'But who would want it?' he asked in a hollow voice. 'Who would be trying to steal it?'

The horseman leaned closer.

'I think you know,' he said, barely above a whisper. 'Who has been disgraced? Who has been exiled? Who has waited for years, biding their time, hoping for the right moment to force their way back into public life? Someone who could only come back through power, not through love.'

A cold dread crept into Harry's bones. His mouth went dry as the realisation dawned.

'You mean – that figure was Cam–'

But before he could finish, the sound of footsteps rustling through the undergrowth broke the conversation. The others emerged from the trees, the Queen Mother leading the way.

'Harry!' Beatrice called out, relief flooding her face. 'Are you okay?'

The horseman pulled back, his expression shifting to something more neutral.

'He's safe now,' he said to the Queen Mother as he lowered Harry to the ground. 'Best you keep him close. There are dangerous things in these woods tonight.'

Without another word, he turned his horse and galloped back into the dark forest.

The Queen Mother placed a hand on Harry's shoulder, her old eyes intense with concern. 'Come now,' she said. 'Let's get you back to the castle.'

Harry followed her, still disturbed by the horseman's words. As they walked back through the forest, Zara and Beatrice kept stealing glances at him, clearly sensing that something had changed. When they finally reached the common room later that night, Harry sank into one of the worn armchairs, his body aching with exhaustion.

'Harry, what's wrong? What happened back there?' Beatrice asked.

Harry hesitated for a moment, touching his scar before answering. 'I think I know who has been disturbing the royal beehives.'

Zara bit her lip and whispered, 'Who?'

Harry swallowed, his throat dry. 'It must have been ... *Camilla*,' he said, the word feeling strange on his tongue.

Beatrice and Zara both shuddered at the name.

'Will and I found the apiary. It was a mess but there was someone there ...'

Harry looked out of the window, calming himself before continuing. 'The thing, the person, was drinking the royal jelly, eating the wax right off the frames. When it saw us, Will ran for it. My scar – I couldn't move. And as it came rushing towards me that horseman appeared out of the woods and scared it off.'

Beatrice and Zara looked at each other, concerned but not entirely convinced.

'But why do you think it was *her*,' Beatrice asked delicately.

'Because of what the horseman told me,' Harry said forcibly. 'He knew about the Stone; he knew about the royal jelly! Do you not think it's strange how concerned everyone is about some beehives? It's not just about some honey ... that royal jelly is special, it's more than just food, it can change you.'

Zara and Beatrice continued to listen, not daring to

interrupt.

'I think,' Harry continued slowly, 'I think it is sustaining her somehow, strengthening her. But that's just for now. I think she's after the Stone of Scone. She wants to use it to make herself Queen – a true Queen.'

Beatrice and Zara now both looked scared.

'But how?' Zara asked, her voice tinged with disbelief. 'And also, why would Philip be helping her? He's been loyal to the Queen all his life. Why would he betray the family like that?'

Harry shook his head, his thoughts swirling. 'I don't know. There's still so much I don't understand. There's so much about this castle, this family, which doesn't make sense.'

They fell into a heavy silence, each of them lost in their own thoughts. After a while, they got up and quietly went upstairs to their rooms. Harry's exhaustion finally caught up with him. He climbed into bed, his body sinking into the mattress. He fell into a weary and troubled sleep.

— CHAPTER SIXTEEN —

Beyond the Bookcase

Though Harry was distracted with thoughts of Camilla and the unsettling possibility that she was the one behind the threat to the Stone, the school year pressed on, and exams loomed over him. Harry wondered to himself what it would mean if she made a comeback, as he sat waiting for his turn at the first exam. Out of everything he had done this year, it was now that he was feeling the most pressure. Everyone had been talking about the exams as 'The Balmoral Test', a marathon of etiquette and protocol designed to distinguish the heirs from the spares.

First up was Smarms.

Mark Bolland beckoned Harry into the room impatiently and asked, 'Why is it imperative that royal couples never commit public displays of affection when on duty?'

Harry, recalling a passage from a piece of homework, answered confidently, 'Because so many royal marriages are built on necessity, rather than love, that couples are unlikely to show affection to each other anyway, so we might as well pretend that this is because of etiquette.'

Bolland nodded, clearly impressed. 'Correct, but always, *always* remember that it is a most important rule. If one day, a royal couple are actually happily married and, God forbid, show it in public, it will expose us all!'

Bolland then observed as Harry completed a set of challenges prepared around the room. One station required him to navigate a medley of one hundred forks, identifying which one to use for each imaginary course. Another station had more of a logic challenge. Using a small model helicopter and miniature figures of the Queen, Prince Andrew, Prince Charles, many young, female potential suitors, and to his surprise, figures of himself and Will, Harry had to demonstrate how all five royals would take unnecessarily short helicopter trips, while adhering to two rules.

Bolland explained, 'No more than two direct heirs can fly together – but also, you must never leave Prince Andrew to travel alone with the young suitors.'

Harry picked up the miniature of Prince Charles, feeling the same emotions swell within him as when he had found the Tapestry of Heirs-in-Thread.

'Yes, exactly,' taunted Bolland, seeing the melancholy in Harry's eyes. 'You, more than anyone, should understand the importance of this challenge.'

Ignoring the professor's pallid, smirking face, Harry completed this task and the others, passing Smarms. But he left feeling dejected and emotionally drained.

Next, there was Tax Fraud and Evasion, supervised by Princess Anne. In the theoretical part of the exam, Harry had to list off the numerous taxes that royals conveniently bypassed: inheritance tax, capital gains tax, corporation tax ... the list went on. But the real challenge came in the practical section. Harry was handed a million pounds and tasked with hiding it in offshore accounts. Harry quickly recounted the well-trodden path through the Cayman Islands, but he also considered Jersey and even the Isle of Man. Time was ticking, and he finally settled on the British Virgin Islands, a favourite among the upper echelons of society. By the end of the hour, he had his million pounds neatly tucked away, and somehow, it felt more like a family tradition than an academic achievement.

His Mixology exam was a different kind of test altogether.

Harry had to recall the favourite cocktails of the senior royals, along with their exact measurements and serving times. He then had to prepare the drinks against the clock. Harry struggled with Princes Margaret's proclivities – there were simply too many to remember, but he knew the Queen's routine inside out. First, a gin and Dubonnet before lunch, then wine with her meal, followed by a dry martini, and rounding off the evening with a glass of champagne. Four drinks, like clockwork, every day. He managed to prepare the drinks just before the time ran out, but in his haste, he knocked a glass off the bar, the shards shattering around him.

The exam finally over, he left the room and Prince Philip's gibes behind him. He puffed out his cheeks with relief as he climbed the stairs away from the cellars but then stopped to rub his forehead. A nagging pain in his crown-shaped scar had been growing throughout the day. He tried to ignore it, continuing his way to the Ballroom, joining the queue for the final and perhaps most mind-numbing exam – History of Majesty. The task: to draw the royal family tree, all the way from William the Conqueror to the present day. The catch? He would lose a point each time the family lines crossed; a monumental challenge given the tangled web of royal marriages, cousins marrying cousins, and a bloodline that sometimes seemed more circular than linear.

After his family tree turned into a knotted mess for the third time, Harry looked around the room in frustration, noticing the same big ears and pasty complexions on many of his classmates. The more he stared, the more disconcerting it became. How related were all these people? He forced his attention back to the page, connecting Queen Victoria to her husband Prince Albert. But then, seeing that he had already connected their names due to them being first cousins, he slumped forwards in defeat, resting his forehead on his crossed arms.

With exams finally over, Harry, Zara and Beatrice made

their way to the shore of Loch Muick to relax. But Harry couldn't shake the persistent ache in his scar or the disconcerting sense that he had missed something important. It was like this doubt had been growing in the back of his mind over the last few weeks, but now the exams were finished, he could not ignore it any longer – but he also couldn't quite make sense of it. Even on this sunny day, as they watched the moorhens on the loch, he had a feeling that something dark was brewing.

He tried to explain his concern to the others, worrying aloud if it was all about the Stone of Scone. Beatrice though, in no mood to worry about anything, urged him to relax.

'Come on, Harry,' she said. 'No one can get past the corgis, and Granny said there are other defences too. Just leave it.'

Harry skimmed his hand absent-mindedly through the cool water of the loch. A small, brown newt dashed out from under a nearby rock and disappeared down into the muddy depths. Seeing the creature reminded him of the evening they had spent in the Queen Mother's cottage, watching the baby lizard emerge from its shell.

Harry's face blanched, and his shoulders tensed.

'Wait,' he said slowly, as though the pieces were finally clicking into place. 'Think about it, Bea. Someone gave Granny exactly what she's always wanted: a Komodo dragon. That can't be a coincidence.'

Zara looked up from her book, with a slight look of foreboding. 'You're saying someone planned for that to happen, that it was a sort of scam?'

'I think it must have been,' Harry said. 'What are the chances someone happened to have an egg with them? I think they planned it, and they wanted something from her. And you know what she's like; she's let slip loads to us that we shouldn't know about. And she even admitted she had been for a drinking competition; you've heard the stories about what she gets up to.'

Beatrice, now also looking worried, said, 'Maybe we should find out who she was competing with, just in case.'

'And' Harry said urgently, 'did she tell them anything about her corgis?'

Abandoning their sunny spot by the loch, they hurried off to the Queen Mother's cottage, bursting through the door unceremoniously.

The Queen Mother was there, lounging in a large, floral armchair, sipping tea with her customary nonchalance.

'Granny,' Harry panted, 'can you tell us about the person you beat in that drinking contest? The one who gave you the Komodo dragon.'

She blinked, taken aback. 'Oh, I never did get their name. They were some charming stranger that I hadn't seen before. To be honest, I didn't really get a good look at them either, they had their hood up, and my eyesight was a bit fuzzy ...'

Harry looked at the others in trepidation.

The Queen Mother, oblivious to their apprehension, continued, 'But after I won, we got talking about pets. I said I'd always fancied a lizard, and wouldn't you know it – they happened to have one. And not just any lizard, but a Komodo dragon! But before they handed the egg over, they wanted to be sure I could handle it. I told them – who did they think had looked after all the animals given as royal gifts over the years? Me, of course!'

She started counting them off on her fingers.

'I've had Marques and Aizita, the two black jaguars given to us in 1986 from Brazil. Jumbo, the forest elephant from Cameroon. There were the two adorable pygmy hippos from Liberia in 1961 and the same year, the Queen was given a Nile crocodile called Mansa. With all of these little tykes, there's always a knack for how to tame them. Like with my corgis – they might look fierce, but they'll obey you completely, if you know the trick.'

'What trick?' Zara asked quickly.

The Queen Mother laughed, as though it were obvious. 'Oh, they'll go for anything rabbit-shaped and be distracted for hours. Simple as that.'

Harry's heart seemed to stop beating. Looking horrified at Zara and Beatrice, they all understood what this meant: someone else knew how to get past the corgis – the Stone was no longer safe. They turned and ran from the cottage, leaving the Queen Mother shouting after them in confusion.

As they raced towards the castle, Harry knew that they had to act.

'It has to be him,' he muttered, half to himself. 'The hooded figure, the one who gave Granny the egg. It was either Philip or ... Camilla.'

Zara gulped and quickened her step as they hurried through the entrance doors.

'*Her?* But why now? Why after all this time?'

'I don't know,' admitted Harry. 'But think about it. The timing, the dragon, the attempts to get past the corgis ...'

Just as they reached a side passage, Princess Anne appeared, her arms crossed, eyeing them suspiciously.

'And why are you three skulking about indoors on a day like this?'

They stopped in their tracks, caught off guard by her sudden arrival. Harry hesitated but finally spoke, the urgency in his voice undeniable.

'We need to see the Queen.'

Princess Anne scoffed, her expression a mixture of surprise and annoyance. 'The Queen? Absolutely not. She's far too busy, and besides, she's not even here. She was called away on urgent royal duties. One of our former colonies want to leave the Commonwealth again.'

This was the last thing that Harry wanted to hear. The Queen couldn't be gone today, not now!

'But we need to speak to her,' he insisted, his voice growing more desperate. 'It's about the Stone of Scone; we think it's in danger.'

For a moment Princess Anne was lost for words, a hint of recognition in her eyes. But just as quickly, she recovered.

'I have no idea how you know about the Stone of Scone, but it is well looked after. I assure you that whatever your concerns are, they are irrelevant compared to the Queen maintaining the unity and the fealty of the Commonwealth.'

Without waiting for a response, she turned on her heel and strode off, leaving them standing there, helpless. They began walking towards their common room, trying to piece together what they knew.

'If the Queen is away, the Stone isn't safe,' Zara said, her voice trembling. 'Philip – he's going to steal it, tonight.'

*

By evening, back in their common room, Harry had made up his mind. He couldn't wait any longer. 'I have to get to the Stone before Philip does,' he said resolutely. 'I'll use the Infallibility Cloak, sneak past the corgis, and figure it out from there.'

Zara and Beatrice were immediately alarmed.

'Harry, you can't be serious,' Zara said, her voice rising. 'It's too dangerous. If you get caught –'

'I'll be exiled,' Harry interrupted, his resolve hardening. 'And I don't care. I've lived most of my life as a commoner anyway. I can go back to it if I have to. But I must try. Someone needs to protect the Stone.'

Zara shook her head. 'But why you, surely one of the senior royals can help?'

'Look at what Princess Anne said,' Harry said impatiently. 'They won't listen to us. If we don't want the Stone to be taken, we are the only ones who can stop it.'

'But Harry,' Beatrice implored, 'what can you do? If Philip is there, you won't stand a chance.'

'Maybe, but I have to try,' Harry answered defiantly. 'This family isn't perfect, and I certainly don't like the idea of Will being king any more than you do. But it's better than Camilla taking over. Can you imagine what it would be like, with Queen Camilla on the throne? I don't know why Philip is helping her, but I must stop him. I don't have a choice – I have to do what's right. I will do my duty, for my family.'

The concern in Beatrice and Zara's faces was clear, but there was something else there too, admiration. They knew Harry was right, even if it terrified them.

Zara squeezed his hand. 'Then we're coming with you.'

They waited until the common room emptied out, the soft crackling of the fireplace the only sound left, as the castle grew quiet. Harry retrieved the Infallibility Cloak from upstairs and tucked the rabbit-shaped toy that the Queen Mother had given him for Christmas into his pocket.

He rejoined the others, but as they reached the common room door, a quiet voice cut through the silence.

'Where are you going?'

The three of them turned, startled.

Peter was standing in the shadows, arms crossed defiantly.

'You are going out, aren't you? You're going to get us all in trouble again.'

Harry's temper flared. 'Peter, we haven't got time to explain, just leave it. Get out of the way!'

Peter took a brave step forward. 'We're Plantagenets. We are meant set an example. I won't let you bring our house into disgrace again.'

Harry was out of patience, his frustration boiling over. He walked right up to Peter, his posture straightening while he drew out his sceptre, and in a voice filled with authority, declared, 'I am second in line to the throne. I am better than you. I command you to step aside.'

Peter dithered, momentarily stunned by Harry's sudden display of royal prerogative. After a strained pause, he relented, stepping back with a look of reluctant and begrudging respect.

'Fine. But don't say I didn't warn you.'

Without another word, Harry, Zara, and Beatrice slipped out, into the silent corridor beyond. The trio reached the East Wing with surprising ease; the castle was strangely and suspiciously empty. Each time they rounded a corner, they expected to find Fawcett, waiting there to catch them, but each passageway was deserted. If anything, the lack of any activity or obstacles felt ominous, as if they were walking into a trap.

As they approached the door to the room with the Queen Mother's corgis, they slowed. They could hear noises on the other side. Turning the handle, slowly, carefully, Harry realised it was unlocked. He leaned in, peering around the door, and saw the three ferocious corgis, famed for their ruthless territoriality, completely distracted. They were tearing apart the remains of a plush bunny rabbit, their little bodies wriggling with excitement, but the toy was disappearing fast.

Harry quickly pulled the mechanical bunny from his pocket. It was wound tight, ready for action. He set it down carefully on the floor, and it sprang into motion, its legs hopping in jerky, mechanical spurts.

'Quick, let's get through the bookcase before the rabbit runs out of hops!' Harry whispered urgently.

The mechanical bunny bounced across the room, and the corgis pounced after it with wild enthusiasm, their attention fully captured. The trio dashed forwards and reached the bookcase, searching for a switch or handle. After a few nerve-wracking seconds, Zara managed to trigger the mechanism, and the bookcase slid open with a low groan.

Before them was a dark, narrow chute. Harry took a deep breath, eager to get away from the sound of growls and springs twanging and jumped into the darkness.

He landed with a dull thud in what felt like soft, dry leaves. A stale, suffocating odour filled his lungs, and he began to cough, struggling to breathe. The smell of nicotine was overwhelming. As he wheezed, Zara and Beatrice landed beside him, sending up more clouds of ash and tobacco, making the air even thicker.

'Oh no,' Zara spluttered between coughs. 'This must be Princess Margaret's secret stash of cigarettes!'

Harry groaned, waving his hand in front of his face in a futile attempt to clear the air. The thick haze stung their eyes, and the acrid smell of stale smoke clung to them. They could barely see each other through the oppressive fog.

'We need to get out of here, fast,' Zara choked, covering her mouth with her sleeve.

Beatrice, rubbing her eyes, squinted through the clouds. 'How do we get through this? Should we burn it?'

Zara gave her an incredulous look and spluttered, 'Are you mad? The smoke would kill us all. And if it didn't, Princess Margaret definitely would when she found out what we'd done!'

Harry blinked rapidly, trying to clear his burning eyes. 'We'll have to clear a path. Use the sceptres,' he suggested hoarsely.

They pulled out their sceptres and with careful swipes, they began pushing aside the mountains of cigarettes, sending cascading waves of crushed tobacco to the side. Fumbling their way through the nicotine-soaked mess, they finally saw a faint light glimmering ahead: a passageway at the far end of the room.

'Come on,' Harry rasped, his voice muffled by the stale air. 'We're almost there.'

Shielding their eyes and holding their breath as best they could, they stumbled in the direction of the light.

The passageway was low; the walls were made of rough stone, trickling with damp. It was slightly cooler here, the oppressive stench of the cigarette room beginning to fade behind them, though the taste of ash still lingered on their tongues. They reached a closed door, but something was odd. From the other side, they could hear faint chirping, the rapid rustling of wings, and the soft whistle of air passing through feathers.

'What's that?' Beatrice asked nervously, pressing her ear against the door.

'Birds,' Zara said, though she sounded uncertain.

'Or bats, maybe.' Harry frowned. 'Whatever it is, it sounds like there's a lot of them.'

Beatrice shuddered at the thought of opening the door to a swarm of flying creatures, but Harry, leading the way, reached for the handle. 'We can't stop now. We need to hurry.'

He turned the handle and slowly pushed the door open, unsure of what awaited them on the other side. Inside lay an unexpected sight – hundreds of songbirds, their small, delicate bodies flitting through a tall, airy chamber. Moonlight filtered through narrow windows high above, casting shifting patterns of light and shadow as the birds fluttered around. It was beautiful, but Harry's eyes weren't on the birds for long. His gaze quickly locked onto a large, imposing door on the far side of the chamber.

'Over there,' he whispered, pointing it out to Beatrice and Zara.

They all eyed the door, wondering if they could get to it safely. But, as they crossed the room cautiously, keeping an eye on the unpredictable flurry of birds, they found the door locked tight. Harry pulled at the heavy handle, but it wouldn't budge.

'It needs a key,' he muttered. He glanced back at the others, who were inspecting the chamber for clues.

'That's a problem,' Zara said, pointing upwards. 'Look at their legs.'

Harry squinted, and his heart sank. There were keys tied to the birds' legs, each one flitting and darting in a different direction. The sheer number of them made Harry's stomach twist.

'Great,' Beatrice sighed, glancing up at the dizzying flurry of wings. 'How are we supposed to know which key it is?'

Harry bent down to inspect the lock. It was large and

ornate, with an intricate design of gold filigree.

'It's old-fashioned,' he said, rubbing his fingers along the carved metal. 'We need one that matches an old, gold lock.'

They all scanned the swirling mass of birds, searching for a glint of gold. Their heads turned in unison as they spotted it – a heavy, golden key attached to the leg of a small robin. Unlike the others, it struggled to fly, its movements slow and awkward, weighed down by the large key tied to its leg. One of its tiny wings was damaged, barely holding it in the air.

Beatrice let out a pitying whimper. 'It's injured,' she said quietly.

Zara looked at Harry, her expression conflicted. 'You're going to have to shoot it down.'

Harry was galled at the thought. The robin, small and fragile, fluttered unsteadily through the air, desperately trying to stay aloft despite its injury. It wasn't like shooting a target or even something larger, like a quail. This was a little songbird – innocent and beautiful.

Harry's eyes moved to the gun rack standing against one of the walls, and he felt a wave of revulsion. He hated the idea of killing it, but they didn't have time to search for alternatives. If they were going to stop Philip from taking the Stone of Scone, they needed that key, and they needed it now. Harry walked to the rack and chose not the shotgun, which would send pellets scattering wildly, but a rifle. He needed precision, not force. If he was going to do this, he had to be sure it was quick and painless.

He took aim, watching the robin flutter about, waiting for the right moment when it was clear of the other birds. His finger hovered over the trigger as he tracked it, side to side. Time seemed to stretch as he focused on the robin's erratic flight. When it finally slowed, moving far enough from the other birds, Harry fired.

The robin let out a soft cry as the bullet struck its already-injured wing, and it spiralled gently downwards.

Harry rushed forwards and caught the bird as it fell from the air. Carefully, he untied the golden key from its leg, his hands shaking slightly. The bird was light as a feather in his hands, its brown eyes half-closed in pain. Guilt washed over him, but he tried to push it down.

He placed the robin gently in a nook of the stone wall, laying it on a soft bed of moss. For a moment, he stood there, looking at its small, fragile body, and thinking of all the creatures that had been hunted on this estate. His heart throbbed with images of quail and pheasants, ducks and deer, all hunted in the name of sport. He wondered, not for the first time, why so many at Balmoral found joy in it. Was this what they felt? The emptiness in the pit of his stomach?

The sharp click of the lock turning drew his attention back. Zara had used the key to open the heavy door, pushing it open with a grunt of effort. Harry gave one last look at the robin before joining the others as they moved into the next room.

Harry blinked in surprise at the sight before him. Arranged around the room, were the six-foot-tall scale models of the Windzors' castles and palaces, meticulously crafted down to the last detail. Windzor Castle loomed at one end, its walls sheer and intimidating. On a nearby corner was the Tower of London, the pale stone of its central White Tower reflecting the torchlight. On another side was Buckingham Palace, stretched out with its grand facade, Holyroodhouse stood stoically, and Balmoral lay nestled in mountain terrain reaching up to knee height.

The whole setup felt unnervingly familiar to Harry, but he couldn't quite place it, until he looked down at his feet and saw the bold letters *GO* painted beneath them on the floor.

'It's – it's a giant version of the Royal Monopoly board,' Harry said, a sense of dread creeping over him.

The three of them inspected the layout, seeing the exit on the far side barred. The realisation struck them all at once. There was no escaping it – they were going to have to play to reach the other side.

As if on cue, a rumbling echoed through the chamber, and they turned to see a huge playing piece, in the shape of a golden crown, four feet across, rolling towards them along a rail. It stopped with a thud next to them on the *GO* tile. It gleamed threateningly in the orange light, waiting for its first turn.

Harry swallowed hard. 'It looks like we have to beat the crown to get through.'

A metallic clang sounded from across the room as a massive chest popped open, the words *Public Funds* etched onto its surface in gold. Inside, the chest was overflowing with piles of money, so much that bundles spilt out and littered the floor. On the underside of the lid, large instructions shone: *Take as much as you want.*

They each walked cautiously forwards and scooped up as much cash as they could carry. It was a staggering amount, but there was still plenty left for the crown to claim, a troubling thought that sat in the back of their minds as they stepped back onto the starting place.

The crown piece went first, rolling down the board with an unsettling grace, moving past the miniature Balmoral and Sandringham. It stopped in front of the model of Buckingham Palace, one of the priciest properties on the board. There was a large sign outside the palace reading: *Pay £5 million in upkeep.* The crown, controlled by creaking, automatic levers, took the money from the Public Funds chest without hesitation.

Harry's turn came next. He rolled the die, advancing carefully along the board. He landed on Holyroodhouse, sighing in relief that it wasn't claimed yet. The price was affordable – a modest £2 million.

They kept taking turns, managing to avoid the crown's properties and, when lucky, landing on the Privy Purse or Sovereign Grant spaces. Whenever they landed on these, they pulled giant cards from the piles stacked nearby.

One read *Royal Wedding Fund: Receive £5 million*. Another

showed *Royal Jubilee: Collect £10 million*.

The game was an exhausting back and forth. The crown managed to scoop up valuable properties, including Windzor Castle and Kensington Palace. But they fought on, holding onto their cash and hoping the crown would eventually overextend itself. Unfortunately, Beatrice's luck ran out. She shook the die nervously in her hand and rolled. She looked from the number on its upturned face to her destination. She trudged, head down, until she reached the space emblazoned with the familiar phrase, *Go to the Tower*. This time she did not have the card that would free her, and she knew her game was up.

In silence, she walked along the edges of the board, past Harry and Zara, until she stood in the shadow of the Tower of London. With her shoulders slumped in defeat, she walked inside the model. As she turned back round, the portcullis crashed down, trapping her inside.

Zara lurched to go help her, but Harry shouted, 'No! Zara! We are still in the game – we've got to carry on.'

With an apologetic look at Beatrice, Harry took his next turn. So far, as well as a couple of castles, he had collected three of the set of the transportation pieces. He owned the Royal Train, a private jet and the Royal Yacht Britannia. Rolling a three, he stepped forwards and purchased the final one: a Land Rover Defender with a built-in roll cage.

The crown's subsequent move saw the tides turn. It rolled forwards, landing on Harry's Royal Yacht Britannia. The sign in front of it read: *In need of refurbishment, pay £17 million*.

Harry and Zara both stood still, expectantly, hardly able to believe their luck. The crown had no choice. The payment cleared out its stash from the Public Funds chest completely. The crown rattled for a moment, the mechanical whirs of the rails beneath it whining and clinking before going utterly still. It was over.

Zara let out a whoop of joy and Harry laughed triumphantly

as they realised, they had beaten the crown at its own game. After hugging in delight, they caught sight of Beatrice, her face pressed up against the portcullis bars, still imprisoned.

'Bea,' Harry began, his voice apologetic, but she waved him off.

'Go on without me,' she said righteously. 'You've got to get to the Stone. I'll be fine.'

Harry turned to look for the door, now unobstructed, the thrill of their victory fading, as the reality of their situation returned. The game was over, but the real challenge was still ahead. They could only hope they hadn't wasted too much time.

Through the next door, a rancid scent hit them like a wall. Harry wrinkled his nose, trying to keep his spirits up with a sarcastic quip. 'I guess we're stinking rich now, aren't we?'

Zara managed a weak laugh, but her eyes were scanning the room. 'I don't think that's it,' she said, pointing. 'I think the smell's coming from that.'

Before them, towering like some grotesque monument, was a giant mound of cowpat, steaming in the torchlight. And beyond it, nestled in the straw, lay the biggest bull they had ever seen. Its flanks rose and fell with deep, rhythmic snores, each breath causing the surrounding muck to ripple.

'Another bull,' Harry murmured, his pulse quickening, remembering the one they'd faced at Samhain.

But this time, they were lucky – the bull was asleep. They crept quietly along the edge of the room, careful not to disturb either the creature or the foul pile of manure.

They reached the exit, and holding their breath, they slipped through, closing it gently behind them. Relief washed over them, but it was short-lived. The next room was unlike anything they had encountered so far.

It was a bar.

Polished, wooden shelves lined the walls, each one stocked with glass bottles filled with shimmering liquids, from deep amber hues to bright, jewel-like colours. The room was filled with ingredients, fruits, herbs, spices, neatly arranged on a long counter. A vast drinks cabinet stood open, filled with crystal decanters and silver shakers.

Harry looked at Zara, who seemed to brighten up.

'A bar?' she said, some of the tension leaving her voice. 'Now this is more like it.'

In front of the counter was a tall, thin podium. A beam of moonlight poured through a round window high above, dancing off a silver serving tray, sat atop the podium. On it lay a note, written in elegant script:

To move ahead and win your way,
A noble drink you must display.
The taste of royalty's in your hand,
But mix it wrong, and you'll be damned.
Beware the drink that leaves you cold,
For Lost Cause is far too bold.
And should you pick the wrong fruit's squeeze,
You shall fall to Fallen Leaves.
Start with the spirit, dark and neat,
From oak-aged barrels, rich and sweet.
Avoid the spice that burns your throat,
For a Knockout Punch won't let you float.
A fruit that's fuzzy, not a lime,
Will help you reach the grandest climb.
But if you mix with too much fizz,
A Flaming Fail is what it is.
Cranberries red, a tart delight,
Will keep you standing through the night.
Yet steer away from bitter bites,
Or Corpse Reviver steals your rights.
Now blend them well, then take a sip,
And on your journey, do not slip.
For if you seek the royal road,

The Royal Flush is your true code.

Harry read it aloud, sounding more confused as he went. But Zara's face slowly lit up with recognition.

'This must be Philip's doing,' she said confidently. 'It's a cocktail-making challenge. We can solve this! We're Windzors, after all!'

Harry handed Zara the instructions and went to the door behind the bar. In vain, he tried the handle, but it was locked. He turned away and perched on a stool, observing Zara with admiration.

She moved with purpose, scanning the ingredients before her. 'Start with the dark spirit,' she muttered, reaching for a bottle of oak-aged whiskey. She measured it carefully and poured it into a crystal glass. 'Avoid the spice ... no Knockout Punch.' She set aside a jar of cinnamon sticks. Zara continued narrating her choices, selecting the ingredients with precision.

'A fruit that's fuzzy ... but not that one – this one, a peach,' she said, grabbing a perfectly ripe one and squeezing the juice into the mix. 'Cranberries for its tartness.' She added a splash of cranberry juice. With all the ingredients combined, she shook the mixer and poured the drink out. She admired her work with pride.

'There,' she said, holding up the glass, which shimmered a rich, red gold in the chamber's soft light. 'The Royal Flush.'

Harry took the glass from her, his hand trembling slightly.

'I still don't understand though, how will drinking this open the door?'

The glinting moonlight then caught his eye. He went back to the podium and carefully placed the glass on the tray. At once, the drink seemed to come alive. The ruby, red liquid glowed in the moonlight, throwing a stream of colour towards the door. The light hit what must have been a sensor as they heard a loud clang and metal arm swung down – a small, chrome device on the end.

Zara hurried towards it and exclaimed, 'It's a breathalyser!'

'I bet that will unlock the door,' said Harry excitedly.

He picked up the drink and looked at Zara; she looked back at him, poignantly. There was only enough of the cocktail for one of them, and they both knew it was meant for Harry. He took a deep breath.

'I'll drink it, then you – you should go and free Bea. Get out while you can. Send word to the Queen. She must know what's happening here.'

Zara's shifted doubtfully. She didn't want to leave him, but she knew he would not be dissuaded.

'Alright,' she said apprehensively, 'but you be careful, Harry. This isn't just about a Stone anymore, is it?'

Harry shook his head. 'No, it's not.'

Harry raised the glass to his lips and took a long, deliberate sip. The taste hit his tongue like a bolt of tonic – sweet and strong, with a hint of tartness from the cranberry. It filled him with a strange sense of calm, and confidence flooded through him. He blew into the breathalyser which gave a happy beep, followed by a sharp click that signalled the door unlocking.

He smiled bravely at Zara.

'Go,' he said, his voice steady. 'I'll be fine.'

With her face pale with worry, she turned and raced away, leaving Harry all alone.

Harry took another deep breath and stepped forwards through the door. Screwing up his courage, he thought he was ready to face whatever lay ahead, but what he saw made him stop dead in his tracks.

Someone was already there. But it wasn't Philip. It wasn't even Camilla. Harry could hear nothing apart from his own, shallow breathing, as he took in the figure studying a large object in the centre of the room.

— CHAPTER SEVENTEEN —

The Woman with Two Voices

'You!' Harry gasped, the revelation fixing him to the spot.

Standing with his back to Harry, his silhouette illuminated by the silver moonlight that bathed him through a dusty window high above, was none other than Piers Morgan.

Morgan turned around slowly, looking at Harry – not with surprise, but with mirth.

'Yes Harry, me! You really are a slow learner. My lessons have been wasted on you,' he sneered.

There was something different about him – he still oozed the same slimy arrogance that Harry had always detested, but now it was sharper, more dangerous. Gone was the simpering sycophant who constantly tried to ingratiate himself with power. Here, was a man who had his goals and ambitions within his grasp.

'But ... Philip ...' Harry stammered, bewildered.

Morgan chuckled sinisterly. 'Ah, yes. Philip.' He shook his head with mock pity. 'He *is* a nasty piece of work, isn't he? But no, he's merely a pawn in all this, like all he has ever been. In a game of kings and queens, he will only ever be a prince.' Morgan spat the last word at Harry with venom. 'In fact, he's been protecting you this entire time.'

Harry blinked in shock. 'What?'

Morgan's grin widened. 'Oh yes, one pathetic little prince looking after another. Remember your first hunt? You had trouble with your gun, didn't you? It wouldn't fire properly.

Well, *sire*, that was me. *I* tampered with it, loosened a few screws, but Philip must have suspected something. He had a look at it before handing it to you, didn't he? And he even gave you extra ammo, just in case.'

The memory came flooding back, and Harry's stomach lurched. He remembered the feel of the cold metal in his grip, how it jarred and injured his hand when he fired at the stag. He also remembered Philip's sly look as he inspected the weapon before handing it to him.

'So – it was you that tried to hurt me?'

'Not hurt,' Morgan corrected, his tone dripping with false innocence. 'Only ... embarrass. But Philip, well, he's not as clueless as you might think. He's been keeping an eye on you, and me, ever since.'

Harry, finally understanding his intrinsic distrust of Morgan from the first time they met, started to piece things together.

'So, it was *you* who let the bull loose.'

Morgan's smile turned wicked. 'Of course. I've always had a talent for bullshit. But old Philip, he wasn't fooled. He knows a false story when he sees one better than anyone.' He smirked, relishing the look of insult and horror on Harry's face. 'Philip suspected that I was up to something at Samhain, that's how he beat me to the East Wing that night, foiling my plans. Too bad those blasted corgis didn't take a bigger chunk out of him.'

Harry's thoughts spun, trying to process everything. Philip had been protecting him. And Morgan – he was the one behind it all, but what did he want?

Trying to sound brave, Harry asked, 'But who are you working for? Why would you betray the royals – you are nothing without us?'

With an angry wave of his hand, Morgan simmered, 'Enough questions. I need to figure this out.'

He turned his back on Harry and looked up at a large object, gently swaying from an ornate frame.

Harry had been so focussed on Piers Morgan he had not

taken in the surroundings of where they were. But now, he saw what Morgan was standing in front of.

It was the Tapestry of Heirs-in-Thread.

Morgan continued to chunter to himself, pacing in front of the tapestry.

'The Stone, it's here somewhere. It must be. Every coronation ... every damn king and queen. But where? Where is it hidden?'

Harry, trying to slow Morgan down, played for time.

'If Philip has been trying to hinder you, then there must be someone else here that you are working with. I heard you ... I heard you whimpering and pleading to someone in a classroom not long ago.'

Harry saw Morgan's arrogant demeanour waver. His eyes swivelled towards Harry, his unpleasant smile failing.

'You are mistaken.'

'You're not as in control as you think, are you? You've been serving someone – just a lowly minion, like always. Who is it?'

Harry thought he knew the answer but dreaded the confirmation. He glanced around, trying to make out any exits in the gloomy alcoves, wondering if he should run. But he had to know. He remembered the night in the forest, what he had seen, and what the horseman had told him.

Morgan's face twisted with frustration. He seemed torn between his instinct to gloat and the need to keep secrets. For now, he continued to examine the lines on the tapestry, searching for meaning.

Taking a deep breath, half to get answers and half to slow Morgan down, Harry prompted, 'Without us, you have no stories, no relevance. Why would you betray us? Why are you trying to steal the Stone? If you are working alone, you are wasting your time, you will fail.'

Piers Morgan's lip snarled. Finally, he spat out the truth, unable to resist the urge to show off any longer.

'You underestimate me child. I have got to where I am

through grift, not by accident of birth. Working for *The Sun* opened up certain ... opportunities for me. I started to see what needed to change, and who could bring about a new order – one that restored the ambitious and the superior to their rightful place. I knew of the one person who could do this. Some thought she was lost but I searched for her ... I found her.'

A wicked smile came back to Morgan's face. He looked hungry and frenzied – teeth bared like a cornered animal.

'It was Camilla who gave me purpose, who helped me see the bigger picture. Meeting her was the moment everything changed. She showed me what I must do ... and I gratefully accepted.'

Harry felt sick, his worst fears confirmed.

Morgan continued, his voice pulsing with conceit.

'For years, I've been gathering stories, collecting dirt on the Windzors, waiting for the right moment. But here's the thing – it doesn't matter! No matter how many scandals I uncover, no matter how petty, unfaithful, or undeserving the royal family proves to be, the public keep on accepting them. They bow, they scrape, they worship. The royals are untouchable!'

He prowled in front of Harry, his hands gesturing wildly.

'My whole career, all the tricks I learnt in journalism, they're pointless when it comes to the Windzors. There's no need to dig for dirt when they provide it so freely. The public eats it up and still treats them like gods.'

He strode purposefully back to Harry, looking down at him with utter contempt.

'But what do the royals do with this subservience? You strut around Balmoral, preparing for a lifetime of *duties*. You live a life of insecurity, forever terrified that one day, the public will lose interest in you. You are wasting such power so fretfully!'

His voice had risen into a demented clamour, the words echoing harshly around the stone chamber and then fading into a cold silence as his eyes burnt into Harry's.

'That's why we need a change,' he breathed in his usual slithery tone that unnerved Harry much more than the shouting. 'The country needs a change; the House of Windzor has become stale. The Queen, the heirs and the spares have become paranoid, pathetic and worst of all – boring. Your family's time is up, and Camilla is the only one that deserves to replace you. She doesn't fear the press, she certainly doesn't fear the public ... but they will fear her. But, for Camilla to take her rightful place, for her to rise as the true queen, we needed something more. We needed the Stone of Scone. The symbol of a monarch's divine right to rule.'

Harry didn't know what to say. But whatever doubts he had felt over the year about some of the pretentiousness and questionable morality of his family's sovereignty, he knew that he had to stop Piers Morgan. He had to stop Camilla. She could not be allowed to become queen, and if it was the Stone of Scone that she needed, he had to do anything he could to keep it from her.

'She will never be coronated. You will never get the Stone!' Harry said valiantly, but Morgan let out a derisory laugh.

'I nearly got the Stone months ago, when it was being kept at Coutts,' Morgan sneered. 'Unfortunately, by the time I broke into the vault, it had already been moved. We met that day, Harry, do you remember? The Queen Mother introduced me to you at the Goring hotel. I should have realised what you two were doing – there's not much that gets her away from the drink's cabinet.'

Harry glared at Morgan who continued to lecture him.

'Luckily, I had my backup plan; I, like you, had secured my place at Balmoral. But it wasn't to teach you insufferable little princes about Deference Towards the Monarchs. No, I was there to be closer to my true queen. To be ready when the opportunity came to steal the Stone of Scone and finally elevate her to her rightful place.'

Morgan focused back to the tapestry, his eyes narrowing in

vexation. 'This tapestry, it's tied to the Stone. But it's not telling me what I need to know. This poem written on it, what does it mean?'

Harry quietly tried to compose himself behind Morgan. He remembered how, when Beatrice had looked at the tapestry, she had seen things he hadn't, old branches of the royal family tree, parts of their lineage that he had not noticed. Maybe Morgan, being a commoner, couldn't perceive the full details of what the tapestry concealed. He then followed Morgan's gaze, reading the stitched words at the top again. *To the righteous and worthy, this tapestry shares* – surely that confirmed it, Morgan wouldn't be able to understand the tapestry's full meaning. *Do not look too closely at the lives that we led* ... and then it struck him, Harry could see something new. The colours, the patterns – they weren't only decorative. They were showing something else, revealing a secret that Morgan could not grasp. Looking at the tapestry as a whole, the lines seemed to intersect, forming shapes and images. But Harry still did not fully understand, he still could not interpret the outlines.

Then, suddenly, pulling Harry's attention away from the tapestry, Morgan beseeched, 'Help me, my queen! I do not understand. What should I see? Where is the Stone?'

To Harry's horror, from the shadows stepped Camilla. Her once noble demeanour had been replaced by a gauntness, her eyes hungry and hollow, reminding him instantly of the creature that had attacked him in the forest. She didn't speak at first, but stood there, her presence suffocating the room, dominating the space with an impending malice.

'Stand guard,' she said quietly to Morgan without looking at him.

Morgan slunk back, leaving Harry and Camilla alone before the tapestry.

'Harry, dear Harry, come here,' she said gently, her voice sweet but with an unmistakable authority. 'I have longed to meet you, and I'm sure you have many questions for me.'

Harry couldn't move. His scar, the crown-shaped mark on his forehead, burnt like fire. In his mind, he heard screeching, like car tires screaming against tarmac, and a bitter, acrid smell of burning filled his nostrils. He could feel it now vividly: smoke, fire, flashes of light. His mother, his father – Charles and Diana – their screams. The agony swelled as he comprehended who stood before him. This was the woman who had come between them. The woman who had shattered his parents' love.

'You know, Harry,' Camilla crooned, trying to diffuse the tension. 'You remind me of your father ... you don't look much like him – but you have the Windzor eyes.'

Harry stared at her suspiciously, wary of her every word.

'I knew him better than anyone,' Camilla continued innocently, 'and I loved him, and he loved me, Harry.'

'Don't talk to me about my father,' Harry said angrily, finding his voice. 'You messed everything up for him, for my family – he would still be alive if not for you!'

'Surely you know, deep down, I would never have hurt him,' Camilla said softly. 'All these years since; the rumours, the lies, the disgrace. Yet the truth is that I was trying to free him from years of servitude and pretence.'

Every bone in Harry's body distrusted and loathed her, and yet, in the way that she spoke about his father, he knew she was being sincere. Feeling very small and alone in the damp, bleak chamber, he looked back at her.

'If he loved you, why did he marry my mother instead?'

'Don't you understand, Harry?' she said, her voice now shy, almost pleading. 'The public and the Palace were never going to accept me. My beloved Charles had to marry someone younger, someone more innocent, more *aristocratic*,' she sneered the last word with bitterness. 'But we were never truly apart. Even when that pretender, Diana, came between us.'

Harry flinched at his mother's name. How dare she insult her; how dare she talk about his parents in front of him like that.

'My mother did not get between you and my father – it's *you* that broke my family apart. You are the reason for it all. I know what you did.'

Camilla let out a scoff. 'You do not know anything. You are a foolish, ignorant child.'

She continued, louder and more boldly, projecting to the room, as if letting out a tirade that had been bottled up for years. 'It is pitiful how little you really understand about your parents. Monarchies, dynasties, fairytales ... there is a fine line between these, Harry. The public know our names, they know our faces ... they know our stories – but that is all they are. You see, the media tells its tales about love and patriotism and duty, and that is what the people see, obligingly and obediently.'

She brought her hands together and swayed with a sickly-sweet look upon her face.

'Oh, sweet Diana, so perfect, so *pure*. The people and the press at last had what their hearts desired, the fairytale princess. But what about my heart's desire? What about me? But, of course, every fairytale needs a villain and here I was, ready to be used, served up, spat at by the underclass, the vermin ... and you dare to accuse *me* of spoiling true love?'

Her lips curled as she directed her vitriol back at Harry, seeing only him.

'Here you are, parroting the same fiction, with no idea about the truth. Their marriage was always doomed to fail – it needed no help from me. Charles never loved her, but Diana so desperately wanted to believe the fantasy, she fooled herself. And then, tragically, she could not cope when the illusion of their confected, romanticised great love began to unravel in front of the world.'

She gave, a leering, saccharine simper.

'Through it all, I waited patiently, I knew that my time, my story, would come – but I would be the one to write it. Once Charles could return to me, openly, we would rule together –

and we would do it right! Why should we live in fear of the press and the public, covering up scandal after scandal? The public should fear us – the paparazzi, the very ones who plagued me for years, should be working for us.'

Harry's fists clenched, the fury building inside him. He couldn't bear the way she talked about his mother and about his father as if she owned him, controlled him.

Camilla's voice lowered again, a dark sorrow creeping into it. 'But fate had other plans. Your meddlesome mother, along with my beloved Charles, died in that tragic accident. Two *were* meant to die that night, but not my prince.'

Harry's breath caught. Could he trust what she was saying? Was she admitting to what the rumours had always suggested?

'Yet all can made right, Harry,' she persisted. 'With your help we can mend what was broken and begin a new dynasty. You see, no rightful heir truly dies,' Camilla whispered. 'Charles' spirit lives on, in me. Royal jelly has sustained us this far, and with the Stone of Scone's healing powers, I will bring him back. They mocked him for years about his faith in alternative medicine, but Charles was right. As long as a small part of him still lives on, he can be resurrected!'

Her eyes gleamed with fervour.

Harry began to feel overwhelmed, doubt and confusion draining him.

'How can that be possible?' he said. 'That's all myth and legend. It can't be real.'

'Oh, but it is real – your father knew it too. His old mentor, Laurens van der Post, shared the secrets of the Stone with him. Together, your father and I, delved into the mysteries and the might of the Stone. During my time in exile, I have planned ... I discovered where it was being kept and how to harness its power. I have had setbacks, but now it is within reach. It is time to use it to its full potential, for Charles ... he will rise again ...'

Her shrill, deranged voice reverberated off the walls.

'And with that miracle, everyone will bow to him, with me by his side,' Camilla pronounced, raising her arms towards the vaulted ceiling. 'Then, the Stone will fulfil its final purpose: the coronation of all coronations. Elizabeth's time is over. It is our time now. King Charles *and* Queen Camilla.'

She closed her eyes in blissful, triumphant euphoria.

Harry looked up at her in revulsion. He watched as she mimed placing a crown on her white, wild hair.

'We have a queen,' protested Harry loyally, 'and you are nothing compared to her! The public have rejected you once and I am sure they would do so again.'

Camilla's eyes snapped back open; her trance interrupted.

'They will have no choice,' she said flatly.

Then, tilting her head, like a cat toying with its prey, she said, 'You do have a choice though. One that you should consider wisely. You're the *spare*. You'll never be king. But ... if you join me, I will make you heir – you will inherit everything!'

Harry recoiled in disgust. 'Join you? Never! You represent everything that is wrong with the establishment. You are not worthy to sit where the Queen sits.'

Camilla's mouth curled in a knowing, sinister grin. 'You say that now, but in time, you will understand. There is no such thing as worthy and unworthy – there is only the throne and those too weak to sit on it.'

'You don't get it, do you?' Harry retorted. 'No one can be monarch without the support of the nation. A real monarch understands the country, its people. A monarch cares for them and in return, *they* grant us sovereignty. The public will never want you – why would they?' he said fiercely. 'You do not know what the people need – how can you, when you think so little of them?'

'Ah, Harry,' Camilla simpered. 'You should know better than that, better than all the other heirs in this wretched place. Like me, Harry, you were brought up on the outside, living in squalor, looking in. You know how the commoners think, you've seen the miserable, worthless lives that they lead. And so, you understand why they need us, why they need to look up to us. The people need a strong monarch, and I shall provide. I shall make the monarchy great again. Restore the true order and rebuild our lost empire!'

There was silence between them, as each looked at the other with more than mere contempt, but outright hatred.

'And now, my patience wears thin. I have humoured you long enough. Look into the tapestry,' Camilla commanded, stepping closer to Harry, 'and tell me where the Stone is.'

Harry stared at her defiantly at first, the growing pain from his scar making it hard to think. He was scared that if he looked too closely, he might see what Camilla wanted him to see. He didn't want to know where the Stone was. But, as he continued to look up into her empty eyes, half-shrouded in her wispy, white hair, he felt drained. He couldn't bear to look at her anymore and so reluctantly, he turned to the hanging fabric.

He looked at his father's name, fighting to keep his emotions at bay. Could he really get his father back, but only by helping Camilla? The thought made Harry feel sick. He looked up at the Queen's name and to the poem once more: *The path to your birthright requires crown, sceptre and stone ... on the way to the throne.* At last, he understood – the tapestry finally revealing its secret to him. The threads of the family tree, when viewed as a whole, made the outline of something unmistakable: *a throne.* And near the bottom of the tapestry, where his and Will's names were, there was the faint outline of a large stone beneath the seat of the throne. It was the same shape and size as the Stone of Scone, the item he had moved with the Queen Mother all those months ago.

Harry's heart thudded loudly, threatening to give his revelation away. The Stone had been hiding in plain sight all along, right beneath the throne in the Ballroom, where the Queen sat during meals.

Camilla turned towards him with a snarl.

'Where is it? Where is the Stone?'

'I'll never tell you,' Harry said, defiantly.

She closed her eyes, a look of manic desperation contorting her face. But when her eyes rolled back open, the white followed by the cold, grey circles, they focussed on Harry with a manipulative glint.

'Very well, if you will not help me, perhaps your brother shall join me instead. From what I have heard, he is clever ... he is cunning ... he is not so insipid as to watch obediently, waiting meekly for his turn. I can offer him what he seeks.'

'No!' shouted Harry. 'He might not be perfect, but he's a Windzor. A Parker Bowles will never sit on the throne.'

Camilla's smile widened, cunning and cruel. Her patience finally spent, she lunged – her long, bony fingers clasping around his throat. Harry pulled at her hands, but they only gripped tighter and tighter, squeezing the air from him. She leered above him, cackling madly and Harry's body began to jerk, and his vision started to fail.

From far away, Harry heard something – a small, muffled voice. It was a man's voice, posh and faltering.

'Gladys ... don't hurt him!'

Camilla's grip loosened slightly, her body jerking awkwardly as if she had been pulled by some invisible force. Harry's eyes rolled into the back of his head, the sound of blood pulsing against his eardrums. As he slipped from consciousness, the last thing that he heard was shouting, snarling, barking. The hands around his neck withdrew and he slumped back, collapsing onto the cold, rough, stone floor.

*

Harry's eyes fluttered open, disoriented by the blurry light above him. For a moment, he thought he saw a small, brightly coloured songbird flitting overhead, its wings casting soft shadows on his face.

He blinked. The gold glint of something – a crown,

flickered in his vision, but as he blinked again, the image dissolved, replaced by the smiling face of the Queen, gazing down at him reassuringly.

'Your Majesty!' Harry gasped, jolting upright. 'The Stone, she's after it!'

The Queen gently laid a hand on his shoulder, calming him with her steady presence.

'It's okay, Harry,' she said softly. 'The Stone is safe, and we have Piers Morgan – he's under arrest.'

'What about Camilla?' he asked anxiously.

Her expression grew more serious. 'She slipped away ... unfortunately we have so far been unable to apprehend her.'

Harry looked around, panicked and disconcerted. It was only then that he realised he wasn't in the dark, cold chamber anymore. He was in the infirmary, and he could feel the warmth of the sun on his face. His head throbbed and as he rubbed his forehead, he paused, noticing a mound of flowers, cards and stuffed toys surrounding his bed.

'What's all this?' Harry asked incredulously.

'Well-wishes from the public.'

'But why?'

'What happened down there was a complete scandal,' the Queen said light-heartedly, 'and so naturally, the entire country knows – apart from Camilla's involvement, of course. I think it best that we keep that between ourselves.'

Harry nodded slowly. He wondered just how long he had been unconscious, especially if there had been enough time for everyone to hear what had happened and even send gifts. Gathering his thoughts, he turned away from the mountain of items and back to the Queen.

'But the Stone, what happened to the Stone?'

'Do not worry,' she said, calmingly. 'As you know, Camilla did not deduce where the Stone was. Fortunately, I came back to Balmoral just in time. As the corgis were cornering Morgan, I got to you. Camilla was retreating but I couldn't follow her

Harry, I needed to attend to you. You had fought bravely, and you were exhausted, ill.'

'Then, where is the Stone now?' he pressed.

'Gone, Harry, to a place from where it shall never return – The British Museum.'

Harry stared at her blankly, thinking, trying to order his thoughts. It was gone, but what would that mean for them? He was starting to remember flashes of the encounter, things that Camilla had said – things that he needed to understand.

Tentatively, he asked, 'Down in the chamber, Camilla talked about the importance and the powers of the Stone. Is what Van der Post wrote about it true?'

The Queen considered Harry for a moment.

'Van der Post wrote many things, Harry. Not all of them are to be believed. However, he was correct about its significant role in coronations. The Stone's place in history is special ... but also its place in the future,' she added meaningfully.

Harry's brow furrowed. 'So – it does grant power? Absolute power, like she said?'

The Queen tipped her head and said, 'The Stone does imbue a certain ... privilege, yes. There are many things that make a monarch; some of those are earned, some inherited, and there are also some that are bestowed. The Stone of Stone, its place in our country's history stretching back much, much further than our family name, is of unique importance in what it represents and what it confers. When used in coronations, you are correct, it grants the power of absolute sovereignty.'

Harry thought he caught a brief glimpse of vulnerability show on the Queen's old, wise face.

'So, if she had found it, she – she could have ...'

Harry's question faded out, partly due to his revulsion of the thought of Camilla usurping the Queen and his family, but mainly because he was remembering what she had said about his father.

The Queen did not answer.

'And what about the Stone's healing powers?' he asked, his voice trembling as he recalled Camilla's full plan. 'Could it ... could it bring back my father? Camilla said, if I helped her, she could bring him back.'

The Queen placed her hand over Harry's. Her eyes welled with sympathy.

'Alas, Charles is gone. He cannot come back.'

Harry's chest tightened as he recalled the strange voice he had heard: the faltering, distant voice that he was sure had been his father's. He took a breath, about to tell the Queen what he thought he had heard in the chamber, but no words came out. Doubt crept in – had he imagined the voice? He pushed those thoughts away, at least for now, and contemplated the one thing that had been troubling him ever since he had been attacked in the forest.

'But – Camilla,' he said. 'She's trying to come back, isn't she? Into the public eye?'

'Yes,' the Queen said regretfully. 'She will never stop. Even with Charles gone, her fate is tied to our family. She has lost her servant, Morgan, but she will find other ways of interfering, Harry. She always does.' Her expression grew distant, as if contemplating battles past. 'You have probably only delayed her for now. But that is all we can do, delay.'

'Can I ask you something else?'

The Queen regarded him thoughtfully. 'Of course. I will answer, if I can.'

Harry faltered, then spoke quickly, the questions tumbling out before he could stop.

'The accident – she said that two were meant to die that night. Does that mean that she ...'

'Ah, that,' she said mournfully. 'I cannot tell you the full answer, not yet. One day you will understand why, but it must wait until you are older.'

Harry was frustrated, but he knew not to argue.

'She said something else too,' Harry continued. 'She said that Will might side with her – surely that's not possible?'

Her eyes softened with a motherly tenderness. 'No, I do not believe that Will, however tempted by false promises, would betray our family. Camilla may believe that she could manipulate Will's flaws, corrupt his honour with the allure of absolute power. But I have faith in him.'

'How can you be so sure?' Harry persisted.

'Because I know my family. You may have noticed that you and Will are quite different. From the time you were separated, your lives have taken quite different paths. As the next in line, Will has endured tireless attention and scrutiny throughout his childhood. But he has also enjoyed privilege and deference; everyone he has met, knowing who he is, and what he will be. This, as I learned when I was young, can be exceedingly difficult to understand and reconcile. It takes time and discipline to know how to put duty before power. Your Uncle Andrew has raised Will in his own image. He has instilled in him the importance of family and status, but, perhaps as he himself was the spare, he has not fully imparted the necessity of responsibility.'

The Queen reached up and took the crown off her head and held it thoughtfully in her hands. She slowly revolved it – the diamonds reflecting the warm sunlight, sending colours bouncing off the walls like a kaleidoscope.

'I became Queen at only twenty-five years of age, but it took many more years for me to truly become *a queen*. There is no shortcut to majesty and those who seek that will fall short. Camilla could never hope to achieve this because she prides positions of power, connections and class above all else, and expects others to do so to. I expect this is what she was referring to when she mentioned Will. Under Andrew's tutelage, Will has developed a certain arrogance, and even impetuousness. However, Will is just a boy, and I have every confidence that he will learn to correct his faults, as I did ...'

She continued to gaze at the crown in her hands, seeing her own reflection in the polished metal.

'We all have our failings, yet it is overcoming these obstacles that helps us grow. To me, mistakes and wounds show bravery and learning, whereas Camilla sees only weakness. And in doing so, she underestimates us. She underestimates Will. He may have his flaws, but he understands the importance of family and duty. He would never betray us and his own legacy to further the ambition of that woman.'

Finally lifting her gaze from the golden crown, she looked back up at Harry, her eyes earnest.

'And just as she underestimates Will, she underestimates you, too. Though you were not raised a Windzor, you embody our nobility and honour – you have proven that today. Having you grow up away from our family was the hardest choice I have ever made, and I have often questioned myself and that decision. But seeing your bravery in thwarting Camilla, and everything that you have done this year, has reassured me that I made the right choice.'

Harry could not help but smile, feeling proud. He had learnt so much this year about how to be a royal, some of it seeming strange to him, but he finally understood what it was all for. He could see why the public adored her. But doubt began creeping back in again – how could he live up to her? And although she was encouraging him, so many of the others seemed unimpressed with him, especially Philip.

'Can I ask?' Harry said, his voice uncertain. 'Why does Prince Philip seem so ... unimpressed with me?'

The Queen chuckled softly, her eyes crinkling with amusement. 'Ah, Prince Philip. Yes, he can seem a bit strict, can't he?' She shook her head with a fond smile. 'But he does love you, Harry, you must believe that. It's just that he cares so much about propriety and the status of the family. He was never happy with you being brought up a Spencer, and so he's been tough with you, trying to bring you up to Windzor standards.'

Harry let out a small sigh of relief. Philip's coldness had always stung him, but he took comfort in her explanation.

'Thank you,' he said. 'That makes sense, I guess. The only time Philip ever seemed to approve of me was when I was wearing the Infallibility Cloak.'

The Queen laughed happily, 'Ah, yes, I'm glad you've made good use of that. I thought that it might give you a helpful confidence boost – help you get into your stride ...'

'Oh, so it *was* you who gave it to me,' Harry said.

The Queen nodded and said, 'It is rightfully yours. It was your father's before you, and so it has been passed down to you.'

'One last question,' Harry said. 'What about the tapestry? How come everyone seems to see something different in it? Do you see Will and me, side by side at the bottom?'

'Ah, the tapestry!' she exclaimed, her tone almost playful. 'Yes, it is a bit confusing, isn't it? But then again, so is our family history, in truth.'

Harry smiled, appreciating her candour.

'Every time one tries to trace their name back to the root of the family,' the Queen continued, 'they seem to end up in a different place.'

Cheekily, Harry pointed out, 'But both you and Philip's lines meet at Queen Victoria, don't they?'

The Queen let out a light, musical laugh. 'Exactly! Which is why it's best not to look too closely at these things. As for your and Will's place in the tapestry – that's not for me to say. Time will tell what princes you both grow to be. Just because Will has been raised as a prince, that alone will not make him a king. He must make the right choices, forge his path, as must you. It is for you two to each make your own destiny.'

Harry felt a surge of warmth in his chest, her words reassuring and encouraging. It was comforting, and yet, it filled him with a strange sense of responsibility.

The Queen gave him a final, tender smile before rising to leave. 'Rest, Harry. We shall talk again, but for now, do not worry about anything. I have everything under control.'

She walked away, her light footsteps clicking on the wooden floor, closing the door softly behind her.

*

The rest of the week passed slowly as Harry continued to recuperate in the infirmary. His aches and tiredness were gone, but the mental weight of it all lingered. Still, it helped when Zara and Beatrice came to visit. They listened with wonder as Harry recounted what had happened – Camilla's escape, the Queen's timely arrival, and the explanations from the Queen afterwards.

They told Harry how Zara had helped Beatrice escape from the model of the Tower of London and got back up to the castle, meeting the Queen as she rushed into the entrance hall, somehow already knowing that Harry was in danger.

The Queen Mother also came to visit Harry. She arrived in her usual flamboyant fashion, but this time her face was lined with remorse.

'I'm so sorry, Harry,' she said. 'It was my fault. I must have accidentally told that dreadful Piers Morgan how to get past my corgis.' She shook her head, clearly upset at her mistake. Her mood brightened, however, as she pulled a large, garish bag from underneath her chair. 'I thought you might like something to cheer you up. I found some things that you can have, to remind you of your mum and dad.'

Harry's heart lifted, until he saw what was inside.

One by one, the Queen Mother pulled out various pieces of overly sentimental, kitschy memorabilia. There was a commemorative mug from Charles and Diana's wedding day, their faces smiling back at Harry. Then she handed him a tea towel imprinted with an image of them on Buckingham Palace balcony. There was even an old keychain in the shape of

Diana's iconic dress.

Harry had to suppress a laugh. It was ridiculous and vulgar but strangely touching. He wasn't sure what to say as the Queen Mother continued piling up the mementos on his bed. He could tell it was meant to be a thoughtful gesture, even if it felt more like an odd collection from a tacky souvenir shop. Still, it reminded him of his parents in a different way – of their public life, of their story which had captured the world's imagination. Briefly, he remembered what Camilla had said about their marriage being doomed to fail. But, looking at the happy faces of his parents, smiling back at him, he dismissed that doubt. They had been in love; they must have been.

'Thank you,' Harry said, smiling despite himself.

*

That evening, feeling stronger, Harry made his way to the end-of-year feast. As he entered the Ballroom, a hush fell over the students. Hundreds of eyes followed him as he walked to the Plantagenet table. The intensity of their stares didn't faze him this time; he was no longer the awkward, uncertain boy who had arrived at the start of the year. He felt surer of himself now, more certain of his place in this strange and ancient world of royalty.

The Queen stood at the head table, ready to address the students. Her voice carried across the room with its usual authority and warmth.

'Welcome all. We have all made it through another year, and thanks to the Civil List, I am sure that our bank accounts are a little fuller. You have the whole summer ahead to enjoy yourself and empty them before next term starts. But be sure to remember,' she added with a piercing look, 'we will not tolerate any scandals during the summer holidays.'

The students chuckled nervously.

'Now,' she said, 'it's time to announce the winner of the House Cup.'

A murmur of anticipation rippled through the room as she

began to read out the scores.

'In last place, with 250 points, is Plantagenet.'

There was a collective groan from Harry's table.

'In third place, with 352 points, is Hanover.'

Modest cheers came from the Hanover table, their banners fluttering proudly above them.

'In second place, with 390 points, is Tudor.'

A polite round of applause followed as the Tudor table smiled in defeat.

'And finally,' the Queen said grandiosely, 'in first place, with 410 points, is Stuart.'

The Stuart table exploded with cheers, Will leading the celebration with an insufferable grin on his face. Purple and silver banners adorned with thistles hung high above them, a testament to their victory.

The Queen raised her hand, signalling for silence. The room quieted instantly.

'However,' she said, her voice filled with a new gravity, 'recent events need to be considered.'

A tense silence gripped the room. Harry looked keenly at her, wondering what she could mean by that.

'Firstly, to Beatrice York, for being the first-ever royal to lose at Monopoly without being a sore loser,' the Queen said, pausing as laughter filled the Ballroom, 'I award 50 points to Plantagenet.'

Beatrice blushed but beamed widely as her housemates clapped her on the back.

'Secondly, to Zara Phillips, for mastery at cocktails under extreme pressure,' the Queen continued, raising an eyebrow as Zara smirked, '50 points.'

The Plantagenets burst into even louder applause. They were closing the gap.

'And thirdly, to Harry Windzor, for protecting the supremacy of the family and the crown,' the Queen said with a meaningful glance at Harry, '60 points.'

The room reverberated with excitement. The Plantagenets were now level with the Stuarts. Harry thought to himself, if only the Queen had given them one more point, they could have won outright. But then, the Queen spoke again.

'And finally,' she said, with a twinkle in her eye, 'I award 10 points for the most important display of valour. Nothing is more important than knowing one's place. It is vitally important to look down on commoners and know that we are better than them, but even more important to look up and grovel to our betters, those further up the line of succession. And so, 10 points go to Peter Phillips!'

The whole room, apart from the Stuarts, rejoiced and celebrated ecstatically. Plantagenet had won the House Cup!

As the Queen congratulated them, servants rushed to tear down the Stuart banners of silver and purple, replacing them with Plantagenet's green and yellow, adorned with a sprig of broom. Harry couldn't stop smiling; it was the best evening of his life.

The next day, their exam results arrived, and to Harry's relief, he had passed well. But, with that, came the end of the school year. Bags were packed, their sceptres were stowed away, and everyone was busy preparing for their departure from royal life for the summer. The Queen Mother escorted the first-years to the nearby village train station, and Harry, Beatrice and Zara gathered round her.

'Now you be good, you three,' she said. 'Keep out of trouble, if you can.'

'Will you miss us, Granny,' asked Harry.

'Yes, a little,' she teased. 'Fortunately, I have my three darling corgis back to keep me company, so I'll be alright.'

As the train horn blared, she ushered them up into a carriage and waved as they were carried away, around a bend.

They settled into their seats, Odette sat in her cage next to Harry. They chatted for a while about what they would do over the holiday, as the train rumbled steadily on through the expansive Scottish countryside.

'You both must come and stay at mine at some point,' Beatrice urged. 'I'm sure mummy won't mind. In a few weeks I'll send Cassandra to let you know the details.'

'I'm sure my uncle will love that,' laughed Harry.

At Queen's Cross, Harry spotted Uncle Charles waiting for him, looking a little uncomfortable. As he approached, he noticed his uncle awkwardly exchanging pleasantries with Fergie, who was there to collect Beatrice.

Seeing Harry, his uncle bade a gruff goodbye to Fergie and held out a welcoming hand.

'Glad to see you,' Uncle Charles said, looking him over carefully. 'I see that you have already been making headlines ...' He grimaced to himself. 'Let's get away from all that, shall we? Althorp will be happy to have you back.'

He and Harry began to walk to the car. Harry looked back at his friends one more time.

'Goodbye, Zara! Bye, Beatrice!' Harry called. 'Have a nice summer.'

Although Harry was sad to be leaving them, and the royal lifestyle behind for a while, he found himself relieved to be getting a respite and eager to return to Althorp. This time, living at Althorp would be different – no longer would he have to tiptoe around, an outsider in his own home, he now knew his place in the world. He was a Windzor but, no less importantly, he was still a Spencer.

Printed in Great Britain
by Amazon